D1514776

THE WORLD'S GREATEST WONDERS

ODHAMS PRESS LIMITED
LONG ACRE LONDON

Underwood & Underwood

GLACIER ROCK—WORLD'S MOST FAMOUS VIEWPOINT

Glacier Rock, jutting perilously from the easternmost peak of the south wall of Yosemite Valley, lies at an elevation of 7,214 feet above sea-level. The rock is poised more than 3,000 feet sheer above the floor of the valley, and commands a magnificent panorama over the wonders of California's National Park.

CONTENTS

F. Henle

THE GIGANTIC BLACK BULL OF MYSORE

The temples on the Chamundi Hill, outside the city of Mysore, are dedicated to a sinister personification of Kali, the goddess of death. On a terrace midway up is a gigantic figure of the Nandi Bull, the symbol of Siva. This huge black sculpture, 17 feet in height, is carved out of a single block of stone.

ASIA

Asia, the eastern, and the far larger, portion of the great land mass known as Eurasia, extends from the Arctic to the Indian Ocean and from the shores of the Mediterranean to the Pacific. Embracing almost one-third of the earth's land surface—it covers the enormous area of 17,000,000 square miles—and holding over half its population—its inhabitants are estimated to number well over a thousand millions—it displays every form of variety, scenic, climatic and racial.

Asia was probably the cradle of the human race. Here was the scene of the world's earliest civilization: here today is the scene of its latest political experiments. Here, too, was the birthplace of the world's greatest religions, Buddhism, Christianity, Hinduism, Judaism and Mohammedanism.

Nature has worked here mightily, and its inhabitants have created not only a storied history but a treasury of art and achievement. Much of this is preserved, in spite of the havoc of many centuries of war.

Turkey is almost unrivalled for its archæological riches: the nine successive cities on the site of Homeric Troy have been excavated, and nearly all the museums of Europe display sculptural booty taken from her territory, illustrating the influence of Greek art in her western regions. Of the ancient and medieval monuments still standing, perhaps the most impressive are the tremendous ruins of Ephesus, the Green Mosque at Brusa, the Seljuk Mosques at Konia and the old Red Walls of Nicæa.

In Syria, the adjacent Levantine country, is Palmyra, Queen Zenobia's capital, a magnificent relic of the Roman occupation. Another such relic is Baalbek, the ancient Heliopolis, situated in the Lebanon, where are the successors of Tyre and Sidon, the cities of those enterprising Phœnicians who founded Carthage and invented the alphabet.

Israel—the Holy Land—is only slightly larger than Wales, but is of world-wide renown as the stage of many sacred events of the Bible. Jordan includes within its boundaries Petra, "the rose-red city, half as old as time," whose rock-hewn buildings are startling relics of a remote outpost of Græco-Roman civilization.

Of the kingdoms of Arabia, the huge south-western peninsula of Asia, the most important is Saudi Arabia, formed by the union of Nejd, the fanatical Wahhabi state of Central Arabia, with the Hejaz, which adjoins the Red Sea and possesses the chief port, Jedda, and the two holiest cities of Islam, Mecca and Medina. Every Moslem who can afford it is bound to make pilgrimage to Mecca before he dies.

Farther south is the kingdom of Yemen, the Arabia Felix of the ancients; and at the south-west corner of the peninsula, guarding the approach to the Red Sea, lies the British colony and fuelling station of Aden.

The Arab kingdom of Iraq, the ancient Mesopotamia, is an alluvial plain between the mighty rivers Euphrates and Tigris. Here was the seat of the remarkable Sumerian culture, centred at Ur, which can be dated back to the fifth millennium before Christ and is the earliest of which we have knowledge. Later followed the empires of the Babylonians and Assyrians, warlike, ruthless Semitic races, who built great cities—Babylon, Ashur, Nineveh, and many others—the ruins of which miraculously survive to this day. The capital, Baghdad, is the fabled city of the Caliph Harun al Rashid, celebrated in the *Arabian Nights*.

THE CULTURE OF PERSIA

Persia—or Iran, the country of the Aryans, as it prefers to be called—is a vast tableland between the Persian Gulf and the Caspian Sea. The ancient Persians developed a mighty culture, relics of which are left in their cities, such as Persepolis, Susa, Ecbatana, and it was in Persia that Islamic architecture in brick and tile reached its maturity.

The region to the north of Iran is peopled by a race belonging to the Turkish family, and is known, somewhat vaguely, as Turkestan. The cities of this region are—or were, before the advent of modern westernizing influences—among the most picturesque and romantic in the world: Merv, Khiva, Bokhara, Samarkand (Tamerlane's capital), Tashkent.

Russia-in-Asia is forty times as large as the United Kingdom, but its population is probably still less than that of Great Britain. A big proportion of the people live along or close to the Trans-Siberian Railway, one of the world's greatest triumphs of railway engineering.

Paul Popper

THE TAJ MAHAL—AN EMPEROR'S LOVELY TRIBUTE TO HIS WIFE'S MEMORY

The Taj Mahal, the most perfect gem of Moslem art, was erected by Shah Jahan, the Great Mogul, at Agra, in 1630–1648, as a tomb for his wife, Mumtaz-i-Mahal, the "glory of the palace." Built by Persian architects in blue-veined white marble, inlaid with pietra dura, it is unrivalled for its perfection of craftsmanship and the beauty of its setting. The tomb, seen by moonlight, is India's loveliest spectacle.

East of Persia lies Afghanistan, an arid, treeless country, elevated 5,000 feet and more above sea-level, with the great range of the Hindu Kush rising in the north-east. On the east, the Khyber Pass is the historic gateway to India. The Afghan cities are small and few: Kabul, the capital, Ghazni, Herat, Kandahar, Balkh. But in the Kabul basin, chief centre of cultivation and civilization, there are many Græco-Buddhist remains to show, notably the rock-cut figures of Bamian.

Equal in size and population to the whole of Europe without Russia, India is a sub-continent rather than a country. Its scenery, extraordinarily diversified, is " an epitome of the whole earth," but its outstanding scenic marvel consists of that massive outcrop of mountains, forming an almost impenetrable barrier across its northern frontier, the Himalayas, the world's loftiest mountain range.

India and Pakistan, with a population of over 390 millions—greater than that of any other country save China—depend at present chiefly on intensive agriculture.

Three thousand years ago India was already a civilized country, with laws and arts of the highest order. Today the land is celebrated for the wealth of its ruling and merchant classes, the profusion of its natural products, the beauty of its handicrafts and the grandeur of its ancient monuments. Of these last, India contains a greater number than any other country.

The old city of Delhi is renowned for its mosques—particularly the vast Jama Masjid—and its Imperial tombs. But it is at Agra that the most glorious example of Mogul architecture, the Taj Mahal, is to be found. Not far off at Fatehpur Sikri is Akbar's famous palace.

It is perhaps, however, in the cities of the Indian States that the gorgeous pageantry of India is seen at its best, for the States are more free from western influences.

A COUNTRY OF SHRINES

Burma is a stronghold of Buddhism and the innumerable Buddhist monasteries not only serve as schools but also direct the life of the people. The great national shrine is the gilded Shwe Dagon at Rangoon, one of the most famous of all temple buildings.

Ceylon, now a member of the Commonwealth, is an island paradise from which our first progenitor is said to have been expelled by way of Adam's Bridge, the chain of sandbanks linking the island with the southern tip of India. It is world-famous for the beauty of its scenery.

Buddhism, of a rather distinct type, is the national religion, and the many objects of pilgrimage in the island include Adam's Peak, on which by tradition the Gautama Buddha left his footprint, the sacred bo-tree at Anuradhapura, the oldest historical tree in the world, and Buddha's tooth, preserved in the Temple of the Tooth at Kandy. The ancient ruins of Anuradhapura and Polannaruwa, and the paintings at Sigiriya, are amongst the most interesting survivals of past ages in the world.

Comprising a vast tableland stretching from the northern slopes of the Himalayas, Tibet, with an average altitude of 15,000 feet, is one of the bleakest and one of the strangest countries in the world. The heads of the Church are the many incarnations of Buddha, of whom the chief is the Dalai Lama. His vast palace, known as the Potala, at Lhasa, is one of the world's most astonishing buildings.

"WALL OF A THOUSAND MILES"

China, the " Middle State," the ancient land of Cathay, has an area almost half as big again as that of the whole of Europe, in spite of the comparatively recent loss of some of its outlying territories. The Chinese have a passion for walls. There is no such thing as a town or even a village which is unwalled, and the whole of the northern frontier is defended by the Great Wall, that great structure over a thousand miles long and more than two thousand years old, acclaimed as one of the greatest man-made wonders of the world.

The Federation of Indo-China includes Tonking, Northern Annam, Cambodia, Laos, Cochin-China and the Southern Highlands of Indo-China. In the midst of the dense jungles of Cambodia lie the thousand-year-old ruins of Angkor, the capital of the ancient Khmers. Its temples and palaces, derived from Hindu art, are among the loveliest buildings in the world.

Japan, or Nippon, the Land of the Rising Sun, is the island-outpost of Asia. The scenery is among the world's loveliest and the temples and shrines, though on a small scale, are elegantly designed and placed in the most lovely spots.

And so we end our brief survey of this mighty continent. Even if her great rival, America, has sights and scenes which Asia cannot show, Asia outstrips her in the wealth of her achievements.

Photos : E.N.A.

A CELEBRATED CASTLE ROCK

Celebrated in the eighth century as the Byzantine citadel of Acroenus, the castle rock of Afiun Karahissar ("Opium Black Castle") rises sheer from the Anatolian plain to a height of nearly 800 feet. From the medieval Turkish fortifications on the top, a marvellous view can be obtained over the mosques, minarets and houses of the old town and across the plain.

BRUSA'S GREEN MOSQUE

None of the many celebrated mosques and tombs of Brusa, former capital of the Ottoman sultans, is more famous than the Green Mosque, so called from its vanished decoration of green-glazed tiles. The mosque was completed in 1423 and is accepted as a masterpiece of Seljuk art. Here is the main portal with its exquisite carving and characteristic niche richly covered with stalactite ornamentation.

E.N.A.

CONE-SHAPED ROCK CHURCHES OF URGUB

In the Cappadocian salt-steppe region of Urgub there are a number of valleys characterized by fantastic cones of tufa rock. These cones, which were formed by water action, have been hollowed out by the monks into cave-dwellings, tombs and even churches, decorated in some cases with crude frescoes. Some of the pinnacles contain several storeys, while rock-hewn steps provide access to the doors.

E.N.A.

STRIKING COLONNADE OF A 1,600-YEAR-OLD TEMPLE

Palmyra, or Tadmor, in the Syrian desert, was in the third century A.D., under Queen Zenobia, the capital of a powerful Levantine state. Amongst its ruins is this graceful colonnade of fifty columns, all that survive to-day of the original three hundred and ninety which were included in the Temple of the Sun.

THE ACROPOLIS OF BAALBEK—
Baalbek, originally a centre for the worship of the god Baal, became Heliopolis (" City of the Sun ") under the Greeks. The Emperor Augustus established a Roman colony here, and Antoninus Pius, in the second century, began the construction of the two great temples on the Acropolis. On the left is

E.N.A.

CROWNED WITH SUPERB TEMPLE RUINS

a magnificent group of six columns, 60 feet in height and a landmark for miles around. This is all that is left of the fifty-four columns of the Great Temple dedicated to all the gods of Heliopolis (or to Jupiter). On the right is the smaller but better preserved Temple of Bacchus, the finest ancient building in Lebanon.

S. J. Schweig

THE STARTING-POINT OF THE MECCA PILGRIMAGE

The Umayyad Mosque at Damascus, 430 feet long and 125 feet wide, one of the most important in Islam, is the starting-point of the annual pilgrimage to Mecca. Originally the Christian Church of St. John the Baptist, it was rebuilt as a mosque at the beginning of the eighth century. The hexagonal fountain in the centre of the courtyard is reputed to be exactly half-way between Istanbul and Mecca.

E.N.A.

D. McLeish

WHERE SOLOMON'S TEMPLE STOOD

The Dome of the Rock (wrongly known as the Mosque of Omar) stands on the site of Solomon's Temple, and, to the Moslems, is the most sacred place after Mecca. Erected in the year 691, it is a graceful octagonal structure, each side 66½ feet long. The dome, 98 feet in height, covers the Holy Rock itself, where once stood the Ark of the Covenant.

THE AKSA MOSQUE AT JERUSALEM

Scarcely less famous is the mosque known as El-Aksa (i.e., "the farthest" from Mecca). It also stands within the Temple precincts and is here seen through the arcade of the Dome of the Rock. Originally erected by the Emperor Justinian in honour of the Virgin Mary, it was converted into a mosque by the Caliph Omar in the eighth century. The porch, with its Gothic arches, however, dates only from the twelfth century.

Martin Munkacsy

THE WAILING WALL

Outside the west wall of the Temple precincts is the Wailing Place of the Jews, who never enter the precincts lest by chance they tread on the site of the Holy of Holies. To this stretch of wall, which is notable for its colossal stone blocks, the Jews still repair periodically to bewail the downfall of ancient Jerusalem.

CHRIST'S BIRTHPLACE

At the farther end of the market-place of Bethlehem stands a simple barn-like structure, the Church of the Nativity, built over the manger where traditionally Christ was born. It is believed to be, in essentials, the actual basilica erected by Constantine the Great in the fourth century A.D. The building with the tower, on the right of the picture, is the Greek monastery.

E.N.A.

D. McLeish

CHRISTIANITY'S HOLIEST SITE

The Church of the Holy Sepulchre occupies the traditional site of Mount Calvary and the Tomb of Christ. Entirely surrounded by chapels enshrining the sacred sites, the present church was mainly built after a fire in 1808. The court, shown here, dates from the Crusades. On the right is the Chapel of St. Mary of Egypt.

ISLAM'S HOLY OF HOLIES—THE KAABA IN

Mecca, birthplace of the Prophet and home of the Kaaba, is Islam's most sacred city, not to be entered by unbelievers. The Kaaba, which stands in the courtyard of the Great Mosque and dates from long before Mohammed, is venerated as one of the earliest temples. It is a small stone windowless chamber with one

Dorien Leigh

THE COURTYARD OF MECCA'S GREAT MOSQUE

door 7 feet above ground, and is covered by a veil or Kiswa of black brocade sent new every year with the annual pilgrimage by the Egyptian government. Fixed in one corner, at a convenient height for kissing, is the most venerated object in Mecca, the Black Stone given to Abraham by the Angel Gabriel.

E.N.A.

THE LARGEST UNSUPPORTED BRICK ARCH IN THE WORLD

Of the vast palace of the Sassanian kings of Persia, built by Chosroes I about A.D. 550 at Ctesiphon, on the bank of the Tigris, all that now remains is a portion of the great hall and the façade of the east wing. The roof of the former, 82 feet in span, is still one of the world's finest examples of barrel-vaulting.

SAMARRA'S SPIRAL MINARET

Samarra, on the Tigris, is a pilgrim resort of the Shia Moslems. In the ninth century it was the residence of the Abbasid Caliphs, and its ruins are of vast importance in the history of Islamic architecture. This brick minaret of the Mosque of Al Mutawakkil dates from about the year A.D. 850, and is notable for its strange external spiral ramp.

THE ZIGGURAT OF UR —SCENE OF THE EARLIEST CIVILIZATION

Ur of the Chaldees, early home of Abraham, was the principal centre of the highly developed Sumerian civilization. Its graves date back to about 3500 B.C., but the Ziggurat, or brick temple in the form of a stepped pyramid, dates only from the New Babylonian Empire—i.e., the seventh century B.C. Its base measures 210 by 140 feet. The shrine of the Moon God probably crowned the top stage.

D. Talbot Rice

E.N.A.

D. McLeish

E.N.A.

MASSIVE RUINS OF BABYLON

Once the greatest city of Western Asia, Babylon came into existence more than four thousand years ago, but the city whose remains are still to be seen on the Euphrates was built by King Nebuchadnezzar at the end of the seventh century B.C. The brick ruins shown here are believed to be those of the great temple of the god Bel or Marduk.

TOWER OF BABEL?

Borsippa, the modern Birs, was Babylon's sister city. This picture shows a mass of vitrified brick, over 40 feet high, all that remains of the ziggurat, or pyramid-temple, of Nebo, its patron-deity. Nebuchadnezzar built it, and Xerxes destroyed it. Local and Jewish traditions associate it with the story of the Tower of Babel.

Robert Byron

WORLD-FAMOUS EXAMPLE OF PERSIAN ENAMELLED BRICKWORK

Isfahan, or Ispahan, was formerly the capital of Persia, and its Royal Mosque, or Masjid-i-Shah, is one of the most famous and beautiful buildings of its kind in the world. Built by Shah Abbas I early in the seventeenth century, it is entirely faced with bricks enamelled in the most brilliant colours and intricate patterns.

E.N.A.

A BRIDGE BUILT BY PRISONERS 1,700 YEARS AGO

The ancient bridge over the Karun River, at the fortified and semi-ruined town of Shushtar, bears the name of Valerian's Bridge. It was built by the Roman prisoners captured with the Emperor Valerian, who was defeated at Edessa by the great Sassanid king Shapur I (A.D. 260) and kept a prisoner till the end of his life.

E.N.A.

TWO-THOUSAND-YEAR-OLD STAIRWAYS THAT LOOK LIKE NEW

Persepolis is thought to have been the royal residence of Darius I in the sixth century B.C. This magnificent double stairway, built of grey marble and adorned with curious crenellations and reliefs, formed the approach to the Hall of Audience. After the Battle of Arbela, in 331 B.C., Alexander the Great burnt down the royal palace in revenge for the destruction by the Persians of Greek temples.

LOVELINESS IN DECAY

The exquisite Blue Mosque at Tabriz, built by the daughter of Jahan, Shah of the Black Sheep Turcomans, was completed in 1465. Its ornamentation of mosaics and its massive yet graceful lines are particularly famous, but unfortunately the whole building has been allowed to fall into a sad state of disrepair. This picture shows all that is left of its finely carved doorway.

E.N.A.

ROCK TOMBS OF LONG-DEAD EMPERORS

Not far from Persepolis are seven magnificent tombs cut in the face of rocky precipices. The modern Persians call the place Naksh-i-Rustam, in the belief that the bas-reliefs refer to their national hero, Rustam. One of the tombs is certainly that of the great emperor Darius I, the rest are probably those of Xerxes, Artaxerxes I, II and III, and Darius II and III.

Robert Byron

THE TOMB OF KING KABUS

There are few more amazing structures in the world than the tomb-tower of King Kabus at Asterabad. From a round plinth, 50 feet in diameter, it is 100 feet to the top of the grey-green "candle-extinguisher" roof. The tower itself is coffee-coloured, with ten triangular buttresses and two narrow bands of Kufic inscriptions. The body of King Kabus, who died in 1007, used to be suspended from the roof in a glass coffin.

FIRE ALTARS OF MAZDA

Zoroastrianism was the ancient religion of Persia. It was stamped out by the Arabs in the seventh century, but is still practised by the Parsees of Bombay. Worship was independent of temples and centred round the holy fire on the altar. The altars shown in this picture are at Naksh-i-Rustam, close to Persepolis.

Photos: Robert Byron

E.N.A.

RESTING PLACE OF ONE OF THE WORLD'S GREAT CONQUERORS

Timur, or Tamerlane, the renowned Asiatic conqueror who carried his victorious arms over India, Persia and Asia Minor, died in 1405 and is buried in the Mausoleum of Gur Amir at Samarkand, his capital. The picture shows the beautiful dome of the Gur Amir, with its unique decoration of coloured glaze.

E.N.A. *Robert Byron*

BAMIAN'S COLOSSAL BUDDHAS

In the red cliffs of the valley of Bamian are cut two enormous figures of Buddha, 174 and 115 feet in height respectively. Inset is a close-up of one of the huge figures which, dating from the sixth century A.D., were mutilated by Nadir Shah's Arab troops in the eighteenth. The surrounding cliffs are honeycombed with some hundreds of caves which were once occupied by colonies of Buddhist monks, but are now deserted.

Photos: Robert Byron

SHRINE OF HAZRAT ALI

Rebuilt in 1461, this magnificent shrine at Mazar-i-Sherif encloses the grave of Hazrat Ali, the fourth Caliph, who died in A.D. 661. The outer walls were completely retiled in the nineteenth century in geometrical patterns of white, pale blue, yellow and black. The balustrades of turquoise pottery are recent additions. The building has been described as a cross between St. Mark's in Venice and an Elizabethan country house.

TOWERS OF VICTORY

The smaller and further of these two celebrated towers at Ghazni was built about 1030 by Sultan Mahmud, founder of the Ghaznavide Empire; that in the foregound by Masud III, his descendant, about 1100. Star-shaped octagons in plan, and 70 feet in height, they are lavishly adorned with zig-zag patterns and Kufic inscriptions, and formerly supported lofty round shafts. The tin roofs are additions, designed to preserve the towers from further decay.

Indian State Railways

CENTRE OF THE SIKH RELIGION—AMRITSAR'S GOLDEN TEMPLE

The centre of Sikh religion is the Golden Temple of Amritsar, 40 feet square, dating from 1766 and built of white marble on an island in a sacred lake—" Amrita Saras," or Pool of Immortality. The upper part of the beautiful temple is faced with copper-gilt plates with inscriptions from the holy book of the Sikhs.

Fox

WORLD-FAMOUS SHALIMAR GARDENS OF KASHMIR

The world can show no lovelier retreat than the Shalimar Gardens near Srinagar, Kashmir's capital. Shaded by trees and adorned with flowers, they are situated by the Dal Lake, against a magnificent mountain background. Jahangir, the Mogul Emperor, built this summer house in the seventeenth century for his wife Nurjahan, " The Light of the World," with whom he lived in the Gardens in the summer months.

Kinsey Bros.

THE KUTB MINAR, A SPLENDID MONUMENT OF VICTORY

One of the world's finest monuments is the Kutb Minar, ten miles from Delhi, erected as a minaret and Victory Tower by Kutb-ed-din, the first Mohammedan ruler of Delhi, who died in 1214. Its height is 238 feet and its diameter at base is 48 feet. Built of red sandstone and white marble, it has a richly ornamented balcony around each storey. The bands are inscribed with verses from the Koran.

Dorien Leigh

THE LARGEST MOSQUE IN THE WORLD

The Jama Masjid at Delhi, the largest mosque in the Mohammedan world, was built in 1644–1658 by Shah Jahan, the great Mogul emperor, creator of present-day Delhi. The precincts, over 100 yards square, are enclosed by red sandstone walls, above which rise three snow-white marble domes and two 108-foot minarets.

F. Henle

MARBLE MONUMENT TO AN EMPEROR'S TREASURER

Mirza Ghiyas Beg was the Treasurer (Itimad-ud-Daula) and Grand Vizier of Jahangir, and this magnificent marble tomb, known as the Itimad-ud-Daula Tomb, was erected at Agra in 1622–1628 by his daughter Nur Jahan, the great Mogul's favourite wife. Persian stone inlay, perforated marble windows and formal gardens add to the beauty of the shrine, which is reckoned one of the finest examples of Indian architecture.

E.N.A.

THE STRANGE PILLAR OF FATEHPUR SIKRI

One of the finest constructions in Akbar's city of Fatehpur Sikri is the Diwan-i-Khas, or Hall of Private Audience. Some 26 feet square internally, its vaulting is supported by an elaborately carved central pillar with a capital of extraordinary form. Four bridges connect it with the wall-galleries. Akbar founded the city as a thank-offering for the birth of his son, Selim, later the Emperor Jahangir.

Photos: F. Henle

AGRA'S SUPERB PEARL MOSQUE

One of the finest products of Islamic art is the Pearl Mosque, or Moti Masjid, built by Shah Jahan in 1648–1655 on the highest point of the Fort at Agra. Devoid of sculptural decoration, it is constructed of white marble and depends for its effect on consummate harmony of form.

AKBAR'S TOMB

Akbar's tomb at Sikandra, five miles from Agra, was completed in 1613 and is one of the most important monuments of its kind in India. The garden enclosure is 150 acres in area. The mausoleum combines Hindu and Moslem art forms in a remarkable manner. The main entrance, seen here, is of red sandstone with marble decorations, while the four tall minarets are of marble.

A MEMORIAL OF BUDDHA'S FIRST SERMON

At Sarnath, near Benares, stands the Dhamekh Stupa or Tope, a stupendous stone structure, 104 feet in height and 93 feet in diameter. It commemorates the fact that here Gautama Buddha preached his doctrine to his first five disciples and won over the King of Benares by his intercession on behalf of a deer. The stupa dates from the Gupta period (A.D. 300–600), and its base is richly carved.

VICTORIA MEMORIAL HALL, CALCUTTA

In the Maidan at Calcutta rises the superb Victoria Memorial Hall, built in 1908–1912 on the site of the old Presidency Gaol and constructed of polished marble. It houses souvenirs of Queen Victoria, historical paintings, statues and busts of Britons who have rendered valuable services to India. The 16-foot figure of Victory surmounting the dome revolves on its base.

Photos : E.N.A.

E.N.A.

BUDDH GAYA, THE CRADLE OF BUDDHISM

Buddh Gaya, which is visited annually by thousands of pilgrims from Ceylon and Burma, is the birthplace of Buddhism, for here, under the sacred bo-tree (a successor of which is seen on the right of the picture), Gautama received Enlightenment after seven years of mental conflict and penance. The pyramidal temple, which dates in part from the seventh century A.D., is 174 feet in height, and contains Buddha's throne.

Indian State Railways

TOWERING WALLS OF INDIA'S MOST FAMOUS FORTRESS

The ancient city of Gwalior is dominated by its Fort, the most famous in India, which crowns a precipitous ridge. Its principal building is the Palace of Man Singh, completed about the year 1500, the picturesque appearance of which is enhanced by its splendid gateways and decoration of coloured tiles—green, blue and yellow. Man Singh was the most distinguished ruler of the pre-Mogul Hindu dynasty of Tomar.

Photos: E.N.A.

THE DESERTED PALACE OF AMBER

The city of Amber, close to Jaipur, is a wilderness of deserted temples, palaces and private houses. The Palace, however, is in a remarkable state of preservation. Like that at Gwalior, which it rivals as the finest example of Rajput architecture, it was built by Man Singh and his successors. When Jai Singh II, the mathematician, chose Jaipur as his capital in the eighteenth century, Amber was abandoned.

PEERLESS TOWER OF CHITORGARH

The Fort of Chitorgarh is the ancestral seat of the Maharanas of Udaipur. Among the royal cenotaphs rises the Jai-Stambha, or Tower of Victory, which is considered one of the most perfect works of Hindu art. Built of yellow marble in 1442–1449, it is completely covered, inside and out, with mythological figures and elaborate ornamentation.

F. Henle

THE FANTASTIC SCULPTURES OF THE DILWARA TEMPLES

Near Mount Abu, the principal hill station of Rajputana, are the wonderful Dilwara Temples. Five in number, they date from the eleventh, twelfth or thirteenth century and are built entirely of marble, which had to be transported from a great distance. The carvings, which decorate the interior walls and pillars of the temples, are fantastically lavish, yet the general impression is one of perfect harmony.

D. Satramdas

THE LLOYD BARRAGE, LONGEST DAM IN THE WORLD

The great River Indus was dammed in 1923–1932 near Sukkur, in Sind, in order to provide irrigation for 6,000,000 acres of fertile land by means of 400 miles of canals. The Lloyd Barrage, nearly a mile long, is the largest in the world. It is seen here floodlit for the Silver Jubilee celebrations of King George V.

E.N.A.

PALITANA—FAMOUS CENTRE OF JAINISM

The peninsula of Kathiawar, divided into 187 small states, is particularly remarkable as a great centre of the Jain religion, founded by the sage Mahavira, a contemporary of Buddha. Near Palitana is the holy mountain of Satrunjaya, 1,977 feet above sea-level. Its summit, enclosed by a battlemented wall, is covered with a maze of temples and shrines, 863 in number. which date from the eleventh century to the present day.

E.N.A. Robert Byron

SIVA'S TEMPLE AT BHUBANESWAR

The Indo-Aryan style of Northern India lacks the over-laden sculpture of the southern temples. Its best-known example is the great Lingaraj Temple of Bhubaneswar, which was erected in the twelfth century. The main tower resembles a beehive and contains a square chamber in which is the statue of the god.

THE BLACK PAGODA

One of the greatest monuments of Hindu architecture is the ruined Black Pagoda of Kanarak, near Puri. This is a richly sculptured Temple of the Sun, built in the thirteenth century. The precincts, enclosed by an outer wall, measure 150 by 100 yards. The decorative sculptures both outside and inside the Temple are amongst the most famous in the East, although the interior carvings give offence to many people on account of their lascivious character.

Kondor Press *Dorien Leigh*

THE STUPAS OF SANCHI

Probably the most ancient buildings remaining in India are the Buddhist stupas on a small hill at Sanchi, in the state of Bhopal. They date from about the second century B.C., and consist of memorial mounds, roughly hemispherical in shape. The picture above shows one of the three principal stupas in the group. Much smaller than the famous Great Stupa, it is 49 feet 6 inches in diameter, and 35 feet 4 inches high to the top of the umbrella above the *harmika*. It is an almost solid structure of heavy, unwrought stone blocks, enclosing a small central relic chamber. A heap of ruins when opened up in 1851, it has been restored, as seen here, out of the original materials. On the left is shown the intricately carved West Gate of the Great Stupa. This, one of four such gates completely restored and replaced in position, is considered to be a structure of the greatest historical importance and artistic value.

Copyright Government of India, by permission of Mr. Arthur Probsthain

A FIVE-THOUSAND-YEAR-OLD CITY

The site of the prehistoric city of Mohenjo-Daro, which means "The Mount of the Dead," is situated in the Sukkur district of Sind and covers more than 250 acres. Five or six cities were built here, each on the ruins of the last. Those laid bare by excavation date from between 3500 and 2700 B.C.

E.N.A.

THE LARGEST DOME IN THE WORLD

The Gol Gumbaz, mausoleum of the Sultan of Bijapur, Mohammed Adil Shah, who died in 1656, is one of India's greatest architectural wonders. On a stone cube 196 feet square internally the great dome, 124 feet in diameter and 178 feet in height, has been erected with marvellous ingenuity. The hall of the tomb, 135 feet square, over which the dome is raised, is 18,225 square feet, the largest domed area in the world.

"THE LORD OF THE WORLD"

Puri, in Orissa, is the sacred city of Juggernaut or Jagannath (which means "Lord of the World"). The great temple of Vishnu, seen in the background, dating from the twelfth century, is built as an enormous pyramid 192 feet high. At the annual festival of the god, thousands of pilgrims assemble and drag the god's

Indian State Railways

RIDES TO HIS COUNTRY HOUSE

image in a colossal wheeled car, 50 feet high and 30 feet square, through the streets to his country house. Stories of wholesale self-immolations under the wheels of the car are pure fabrication, though accidents have occurred and many frenzied worshippers in the enormous crowds have been crushed to death.

K. Johnston

PAINTED CAVE-TEMPLES MORE THAN 2,000 YEARS OLD

Hewn in the rocky cliff of a great ravine are the Caves of Ajanta, formerly a great centre of Buddhist worship. Dating from the second century B.C. to the fifth A.D., they accommodated twenty-four monasteries and five temples. The famous wall paintings in the interior depict the life and miracles of Buddha.

Kondor Press

A VAST TEMPLE CARVED FROM THE SOLID ROCK

The Cave-Temples of Ellora date back to 1000 B.C. and were excavated by Buddhists, Hindus and Jains. A wonderwork of Hindu sculpture is the Kailas Temple to Siva, dating from about A.D. 730–755. Measuring 276 by 154 feet, and 108 feet high, it is entirely carved out of the tufa rock of a hillside.

KARLI'S ROCK TEMPLE

The Buddhist Cave Temple of Karli, dating from the first century B.C., is the finest of its kind in India. Built in the same manner as a Christian church with porch and nave, it is 124 feet long and 45 feet wide internally. The incense-blackened roof of teak beams is 46 feet high and is supported by thirty side pillars, each surmounted by the delicately carved figure of an elephant.

THE SEVEN PAGODAS

One of India's most remarkable ruin sites is in a remote spot at Mahabalipuram, near Madras. The oldest buildings here are the so-called Seven Pagodas, consisting of five small shrines of Dravidian type together with admirably sculptured figures of an elephant and a lion. These figures all date from the seventh century A.D.

E.N.A.

Dorien Leigh

Kingdon Ward

NATIVE BRIDGE BUILDING

The broad and boisterous rivers of north-east Assam make formidable obstacles to transport and communications, but the local tribes display immense ingenuity and no little engineering skill in surmounting them. This astonishing tubular bridge proves their abilities. Of enormous length, it is constructed entirely of pieces of cane held in place by a series of hoops and attached at each end to convenient trees by ropes. Its open structure protects it against high winds and, despite its fragile appearance, it is of great strength and durability.

TANJORE'S SUPERB TEMPLE

The great Brihadiswaraswami Temple at Tanjore is the most outstanding of all Dravidian Temples. Dedicated to Siva, it was founded by Rajaraja I, who died in 1012, ruler of the powerful Chola Empire. The tower-pyramid, 197 feet in height, is crowned by an enormous round stone estimated to weigh 7 tons, which was raised to its position by means of a mile-long ramp.

E.N.A.

F. Henle

A 2,000-YEAR-OLD STONE GIANT

Near the town of Sravana Belgola, in the state of Mysore, on the rocky hill of Indrabetta, is this colossal figure of Gomata Raya, the Jainist sage. Erected probably by Chamunda Raya, it is over 70 feet in height. The sage is portrayed in deep meditation and plants climb around him unnoticed. Although the image is possibly 2,000 years old, its stone has been marvellously preserved by frequent washings.

F. Henle

TEMPLE WHOSE WALLS ARE ALL SCULPTURES

Perhaps the most strange of all Hindu temples is the Great Temple of Madura. The two tower-pyramids (gopurams), dedicated one to Siva (here called Sundareswar), the other to the fish-eyed goddess Minakshi, are entirely covered with mythological sculptures and painted in gaudy colours. The temple measures 847 feet long by 729 feet wide, and part of the courtyard of the lotus lake is shown here in the foreground.

Dorien Leigh

SUNLIT SPLENDOUR OF RAMESWARAM'S MIGHTY CORRIDORS

The magnificent temple in Rameswaram, one of the holiest cities of Hinduism, is much frequented by pilgrims. The temple, which dates from the sixteenth or seventeenth century, is probably the most perfect specimen in existence of the mason's art in the Dravidian style. Its chief features are the pillared halls, nearly 4,000 feet long, and the effect of their interminable sculptures is almost overpowering.

Photographic Publications

A BEAUTIFUL RELIC HOUSE AT POLONNARUWA

The ruins of Polonnaruwa, which was the royal residence from the eighth to the mid-thirteenth century, vie in interest with those of Anuradhapura. Here is the Wata Dagoba, or Round Relic House, a curious circular structure built on a mound and 58 feet in diameter. It is approached by a flight of steps flanked by Dvarpals (doorkeepers with the nine-headed snake) with a beautifully carved moonstone at the foot.

E.N.A.

THE COLOSSAL BUDDHA OF AN ANCIENT CITY

Another feature of the deserted city of Polonnaruwa, which was at the height of its glory in the twelfth century, is the rock temple known as the Gal Vihara, which has three colossal figures, all hewn out of the solid granite. The recumbent Buddha, seen here amid the ruins, is no less than 46 feet long.

KANDY'S TEMPLE OF THE TOOTH

At Kandy, the former capital of the Sinhalese Kingdom, is the famous Temple of Dalada Maligawa, or Temple of the Sacred Tooth of Buddha, founded in the fourteenth century and still one of the holy places of Buddhism. The octagonal tower contains the costly jewelled shrine of the holy tooth, which is over $1\frac{1}{2}$ inches long and $\frac{1}{3}$ inch thick.

DESERTED RUINS OF ANURADHAPURA

The oldest seat of the Sinhalese Kingdom was Anuradhapura, which, though a holy city of Buddhism, has been deserted since the twelfth century and is one of the most remarkable ruin sites in the world. The Isurumuniya Rock Temple, shown in part below, is a most extraordinary construction, dating from about 300 B.C., though it has been restored and partly rebuilt.

Photos: E.N.A.

THE BELL-LIKE SHWE DAGON, BUDDHISM'S HOLY OF HOLIES

The Shwe Dagon Pagoda at Rangoon, where eight hairs from Buddha's head are preserved, is the principal shrine of Buddhism. Completed in 1564, it stands on two terraces 166 feet above the ground, and is 367 feet high; its base is a quarter of a mile in circumference. The whole structure is regilded every twenty-five years at a cost of over £30,000. At the top are hung 1,500 little bells of gold and silver.

E.N.A.

HUGE TOWER OF MANDALAY'S FAMOUS PALACE

Mandalay was the capital of Burma from 1857 to 1885 only. King Mindon Min, who founded it, transferred thither the royal palace from Amarapura and his successor, Thibaw, enlarged it. It stands in the very centre of the old fort. A fantastic wooden structure on a 6-foot platform, gleaming with gilding and colour, it is covered with carving. The tower, 256 feet high, was designed as "The Centre of the World."

A CARVED STALAGMITE

On the Attaran River, ten miles from Moulmein, are the celebrated Farm Caves, hollowed out of the sandstone mountains. With infinite labour, these have been converted into Buddhist rock-temples. The huge stalagmite shown here is entirely covered with tiny images of the Buddha on his throne and on the top is an exquisite little pagoda.

A FAMOUS BURMESE PAGODA

The Ananda Pagoda at Pagan is one of the finest and largest buildings in Burma. It is built round a vast central tower 200 feet square, and each of the projecting wings is 80 feet long. The tower rises in seven storeys to a height of 183 feet. In the rear of each wing is an artificially lighted niche, in which stands a statue of Buddha over 30 feet high.

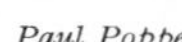

Paul Popper

E.N.A.

THE KYAIK-HTI-YO PAGODA ON ITS AERIAL PERCH

Crowning the northern summit of the Kelasa hills, in the Shwegyin district, and 3,650 feet above sea-level, is the Kyaik-hti-yo Pagoda, which can be reached only by means of ladders. It has been built precariously on the very top of a huge boulder which is locally supposed to be miraculously balanced by a hair from the head of Buddha. Geologists, on the other hand, maintain that it was deposited here by a glacier.

THE "FORBIDDEN" CITY OF LHASA WITH

Lhasa, Tibet's capital, lies 11,830 feet above sea-level, which is considered low-lying for Tibet, and its name means "Abode of the Gods." It is dominated by the famous Potala, one of the most magnificent palaces in the world, dating for the most part from the seventeenth century and some 900 feet in length. This is the fortress-palace of the Dalai Lama, Buddha's living incarnation, secular ruler of the country

E.N.A.

THE IMMENSE PALACE OF THE POTALA

and supreme pontiff of the Lamaist religion. His actual residence, in the centre of the vast complex of buildings, is painted red. In the centre of the lower city is the Chokang, or cathedral, where the National Assembly of monastic representatives meets, and a fine avenue flanked with walled pleasure grounds ascends thence to the Potala. Lhasa is a forbidden city to Europeans, few of whom have ever visited it.

W. F. Taylor

GUARDING THE TRADE ROUTES OF FAR TIBET

One of the most historic fortresses in old Tibet is that known as Gyantse Jong, crowning a great rock, around the base of which nestles the important town of Gyantse, the principal mart for trade between India and Tibet. On the extreme left of this picture, part of the monastery with its wall can be seen.

D. Carruthers

ONE OF THE FAR EAST'S MOST ROMANTIC HIGHWAYS

Sinkiang, the "New Territory," is one of the most remote quarters of the world. Its greatest—in fact, its only—real highway is the romantic Sinkiang Imperial Road, running from Kansi to Urumchi (the northern capital) and Kulja. This stretch of it runs beside the shore of the great Ebi Nor Lake.

Robert Byron

GRACE IN STONE—THE MANCHU TEMPLE AT MUKDEN

This exquisitely graceful stone temple stands just inside the entrance to the Manchu tombs at Mukden. The tombs, amongst the most celebrated monuments in all China, commemorate the Manchu dynasty which in the seventeenth century issued from Mukden, former capital of Manchuria, to conquer China.

Robert Byron

THE GATEWAY OF THE MANCHU TOMBS

This picture shows the superb seventeenth-century gateway giving access to the mausoleum of Tatsung at Peilung, part of the magnificent tombs erected by the celebrated Manchu emperors of China in honour of their ancestors. The luxuriant growth of mistletoe on the trees in the foreground is noteworthy.

Akademia

A SUMMER RESIDENCE OF CHINA'S PAST EMPERORS

The Manchu emperors of China had a summer residence at Jehol, a town about 130 miles north-east of Peking, which they used mainly in the autumn when journeying to the great hunting grounds beyond the city. The surrounding country was all once an imperial reserve, but was later opened up for agricultural use. The famous Round Temple (above) is only one of the numerous temples to be found in the district.

E.N.A.

THE TEMPLE OF HEAVEN, MOST FAMOUS OF CHINESE SHRINES

The Confucian Temple of Heaven, in Peking, was built by the Emperor Yung-lo in 1420, fifty-two years after the revolt against the Mongols had restored the native Ming dynasty. Everything in it is circular to accord with the shape of the heavens. The only person to use the Temple was the Emperor who formally attended every New Year's Day. The three roofs are covered with blue-glazed tiles.

Robert Byron

THE LOVELY GATEWAY OF THE HALL OF THE CLASSICS

This marvellous gateway, faced with glazed tiles of chaste colouring and ornamentation, leads to the Hall of the Classics in the Old University of Peking, where the Emperor himself used to preside over the examinations. No spot in Peking is more tinged with the exquisite Chinese spirit of restful beauty.

A GIGANTIC INCENSE-BURNER

The Lama Temple at Peking is the city's principal centre for the Lamaist cult. Built at the beginning of the eighteenth century, it originally served as the palace of the Emperor Yung-cheng. The bronze incense-burner which stands within its precincts is 14 feet in height and is chased in the typically elaborate designs.

E.N.A.

AN EMPEROR'S TOY

The summer palace of the Chinese emperors, outside the walls of Peking, is known as I-ho-yuan, the "Park of the Peaceful Age." On its artificial lake "floats" the famous marble barge or houseboat, which dates from the eighteenth century and served the imperial family as a cool summerhouse. The superstructure is of wood.

T. Butler

A MIGHTY WALL TWENTY-TWO CENTURIES

The Great Wall of China, the " Wall of a Thousand Miles," is one of the world's greatest structures and the earliest surviving architectural monument in the country. It was begun in the third century B.C. by the Emperor Shih Huang Ti, as a protection for his northern frontier against the nomadic tribes.

Paul Popper

OLD AND OVER 1,400 MILES IN LENGTH

Constructed of earth and stone with a facing of bricks, it is 1,400 miles in total length and is defended at intervals by square watch-towers. It varies in height from 20 to 35 feet, and in width from 10 to 13 feet. Many thousands of the workers by whose labours it was built were buried within its ramparts.

Photos : E.N.A.

PEKING'S HISTORIC LAMA TEMPLE

Situated in the north-east corner of the inner or Tartar city of China's former capital is one of the most famous buildings in the country, the Lama Temple. Among its chief architectural features are the Hall of Prayer, where the monks perform their devotions, the Temple of the Great Buddha and numerous ornamental gateways and staircases.

DRUMS OF STONE

The Temple of Confucius, where the Emperor used to offer incense twice a year to the spirit of the great sage, is outstanding among the buildings of Peking for its solemn repose and simple dignity. The celebrated stone drums, which repose in the lovely Bell Terrace, seen in this picture, have inscriptions dating from a thousand years before Christ.

Paul Popper

MAGNIFICENT RESTING PLACE OF A LAMA'S ROBES

The Yellow Temple, one of the great sights of Peking, is a centre of the Lamaist cult, and was rebuilt in the seventeenth century. This " dagoba " within the precincts was erected by the Emperor Chien-lung in 1780 over the robes of a Teshi-Lama who died in Peking of small-pox. His body was sent back to Tibet.

THE STRANGE HALL OF THE

Canton, lying on the northern bank of the estuary of the Si-Kiang, is the great commercial metropolis of Southern China. Among its numerous religious establishments one of the best known is the Monastery of the Flowery Forest, where, in the Wa-Lum Temple, or Temple of the Five Hundred Genii, a strange sight is seen—a hall filled with 500 seated figures set up in honour of Buddha and his five hundred disciples. This

E.N.A.

FIVE HUNDRED GENII AT CANTON

view shows some of these statues, each of which is a masterpiece of lifelike carving. The Buddhist religion has no priests or clergy properly so called, and the only duty of the mendicant monks is to read aloud the scriptures. The principal ceremony at the temples consists in the offering of flowers, fruit and incense to the statues and relics of Buddha, accompanied by prayers and the chanting of hymns.

Paul Popper

THE NOBLE GATEWAY TO THE TOMBS OF THE MING EMPERORS

From 1368 to 1644 China was governed by the emperors of the Ming dynasty, whose tombs, about 40 miles from Peking, are thirteen in number and provide one of the most impressive sights in the country. The entrance to the tomb area is by a magnificent "pai-lou," or gateway, built of white marble in 1541.

F. Henle

MARBLE ANIMALS THAT WATCH OVER THE MING TOMBS

The approach to the Ming Tombs is by a Sacred Way lined with thirty-two colossal figures of animals (lions, rams, camels, elephants, fabulous monsters, horses) and mandarins, each carved with astonishing ingenuity out of a single block of marble and dating from the early part of the fifteenth century.

E.N.A. T. Butler

THE TOMB OF CHINA'S "SAVIOUR"

This stately and impressive building on Purple Hill, near Nanking, comprises the tomb and memorial of Dr. Sun Yat-sen, Father of the Chinese Republic, who died in 1925. It was largely through his influence that the Manchu dynasty was dethroned in 1912, and he was chosen as the first President of the new republic. His tomb has been a place of pilgrimage for millions of Chinese men and women.

THE ENORMOUS PAGODA AT HANGCHOW

Near Hangchow, the "City of Heaven," on the bank of the Chien-tang River, stands the Pagoda of the Six Harmonies. Founded in A.D. 971, it was rebuilt in 1894, after destruction by the rebels in 1862. It is a brick structure of thirteen storeys, hexagonal in plan, 334 feet high, and each of its sides measures 48 feet in width.

E.N.A.

THE RED LACQUER BRIDGE OF NIKKO

The sacred Red Lacquer Bridge spanning the Daiya-gawa at Nikko was erected in the seventeenth century and restored in 1907 after a flood. Some 83 feet long and 18 feet wide, it rests on granite pillars shaped like "torii." With its black metal fastenings and gilded pinnacles, it makes a magnificent splash of colour amid the green of the foliage, and it is universally acclaimed as one of the great sights of Japan.

Lubinski

THE OI RAILWAY BRIDGE, A TECHNICAL WONDER OF THE WORLD

The railway from Tokyo to Osaka crosses the Oi River near Shimada by a remarkable steel bridge of sixteen spans, supported by cylindrical brick wells and 3,332 feet in total length. It is notable in that its construction is specially designed to withstand the devastating floods to which the river is subject.

F. Henle

THE BRONZE BUDDHA OF KAMAKURA

This Daibitsu, or colossal representation of the supreme Buddha under the name of Amida, set in beautiful country, is considered the finest in Japan. Cast of one-inch bronze plates in A.D. 1252, it is over 40 feet in height, with a weight of about 92 tons. The eyes are of gold, the forehead boss of silver.

E.N.A.

THE OLDEST WOODEN PAGODA IN THE WORLD

At Nara, the ancient capital, is the Horyu-ji Temple, founded A.D. 607, the oldest Buddhist fane in the country. Its time-battered wooden pagoda of five storeys is a harmony in red and yellow, squat with wide eaves, and crowned with a bronze lightning-and-demon-arrester. The ground floor has been fitted up for use as a chapel.

NIKKO'S MOST SACRED SHRINE

The Tosho-gu Shrine, seen here, is dedicated to Iyeyasu and Iyemitsu, the famous shoguns of the Tokugawa dynasty. The stone temple lanterns in the courtyard are votive offerings. At the head of the terrace is the Yomei-mon, or principal gateway, built in the seventeenth century, which is among the most famous of temple gateways in Japan.

Dorien Leigh

E.N.A.

THE GREAT TORII OF MIYAJIMA

Of all the torii, those gate-like structures for which Japan is celebrated, none is better known than that which is attached to the temple on the sacred island of Miyajima. Constructed in 1875, it measures 44 feet high and 73 feet wide. Its base is washed daily by the tidal waters. Torii are the sign of a Shinto shrine.

E.N.A. F. Henle

NARA'S TEMPLE OF LANTERNS

The Kasuga no Miya at the old city of Nara is a highly venerated Shinto shrine, founded A.D. 767 and situated in a beautiful deer park. It is painted a glowing vermilion and possesses many hundreds of bronze or stone lanterns, all of which were presented by distinguished visitors and are lighted up on special occasions.

THE GREAT BELL OF KYOTO

Weighing 63 tons and measuring 14 feet in height, 9 feet in diameter and 9 inches in thickness, the Great Bell of Kyoto was cast in 1614 by order of Hideyoshi, the great military chieftain. It hangs in the Chion-in Temple, and is numbered among the world's greatest bells. Its deep and sonorous voice can still be heard for many miles around.

E.N.A.

THE FOUR-FACED TOWERS OF ANGKOR-THOM

The ruins of the temples and palaces of Angkor, built by the ancient Khmers in the ninth and subsequent centuries A.D., are undoubtedly among the world's most remarkable sights. This picture shows the extraordinary towers of the Bayon Temple at Angkor Thom. Each has four walls, and each of these carries a face carved carefully in its stone. Thus are depicted the four faces of Brahma.

E.N.A.

THE GIGANTIC TEMPLE OF ANGKOR-VAT

The enormous temple of Angkor-Vat, consecrated to the worship of Buddha, is the best-preserved example of Khmer architecture and one of the most grandiose buildings on earth. With its great pyramidal towers mirrored in the wide moats, it rises in three distinct stages and every flat surface is adorned with carving.

D. McLeish

THE ASTOUNDING BALUSTRADES OF ANGKOR

Among the most impressive sculptures of Angkor are the balustrades of the causeway across the moat. These take the form of demigods or demons holding the seven-headed sacred snake Naga in their arms. All the carvings of Angkor are executed in brown limonite or grey sandstone, without the use of mortar.

E.N.A.

THE FAR-FAMED BEAUTIES OF ALONG BAY

Along Bay lies between the mouths of the Red River and the frontier of China in the extreme north of the Viet-Nam province of Tongking. Although such a remote spot is seldom visited, those who have been there declare that for colouring and rugged outline its coast is among the most picturesque in the world.

E.N.A.

BANGKOK'S FINEST TEMPLE

The Wat Chang, the Buddhist temple which towers above the west bank of the River Menam in the Siamese capital, consists of a central " phra-prang," 300 feet in height, with four smaller ones around it. The whole of the structure is faced with a glittering and brilliantly coloured mosaic of Chinese porcelain.

E.N.A.

THE FAMOUS "EMERALD BUDDHA" TEMPLE AT BANGKOK

In one corner of the palace quarter of Bangkok is the Wat Phra Keo, the most richly adorned of all the Siamese "wats" (centres of the Buddhist cult). On the left is the finely carved "Bot," housing the Emerald Buddha, a figure really executed in jade. On the right is a temple with a "phra-prang" (relic tower).

GROTESQUE TEMPLE GUARDIANS

Perhaps the most celebrated of the numerous temples of the Wat Po, which is Bangkok's principal assemblage of Buddhist shrines, is the quaint little Wat Aroon, with its triple saddleback roof and its tapering spire. Its entrance is guarded by two gigantic doorkeepers in medieval panoply.

Photos: Siamese Embassy

EUROPEAN ENGINEERING IN AN ORIENTAL CAPITAL

Bangkok, the Siamese capital, had no bridge across the River Menam until 1932. In that year the Memorial Bridge, of a purely European type, was opened in commemoration of the 150th anniversary of the foundation of the present royal dynasty. This is how it appears from the east or Bangkok bank of the river.

E.N.A.

THE GREAT BRONZE BUDDHA OF AYUTHIA

From 1350 till its destruction by the Burmese in 1767, Ayuthia (" the invincible ") was the capital of Siam. The ruins of the ancient city, now overgrown with jungle, cover an area nine miles in circumference. Ruined palaces, pagodas and colossal sculptures still testify to its ancient importance. This huge bronze Buddha, perhaps the most remarkable of all the sculptures there, has had its right arm restored,

Fox

THE STRANGE GALLERY OF THE BUDDHAS AT THE WAT PO

The largest of the Bangkok temple enclosures is the Wat Po, furnished with innumerable temples, shrines and shady courtyards. One of the chief features of the principal temple is a kind of cloister containing a row of seated figures of Buddha, all of identical pattern and all gilded. The Siamese are enthusiastic adherents of orthodox Buddhism, most men entering the priesthood for at least three months.

THE MARVELLOUS BAS-RELIEFS OF THE

Boroboedoer, on the large island of Java, is the most famous ancient monument in the Malay Archipelago. Probably dating from the eighth century A.D. and perhaps erected by immigrants from India, it rises in a terraced pyramid to a height of 100 feet above the hill whose summit it crowns. The building material

E.N.A.

BUDDHIST TEMPLE OF BOROBOEDOER

is a hard trachyte, and no cement whatever was used. Around the galleries that encircle the temple runs a double frieze of bas-reliefs, numbering over 1,500 slabs and comparable in execution and design to the finest products of classical art. They depict the life of Buddha, and their preservation is remarkable.

G. Heurlin

A TRIUMPH OF MODERN CIVIC ARCHITECTURE

Stockholm's new Town Hall, built entirely of brick to the design of Ragnar Ostberg, was completed in 1923. By many authorities it is claimed as probably the most striking modern building in the world. The great tower, flanked by two exquisitely proportioned wings, has inspired architects everywhere.

EUROPE

SINCE the beginning of the Christian era, Europe has climbed steadily to pre-eminence amongst the world's continents. It won its position at the expense of Asia, for in the pre-Christian era, and for many centuries later, the centres of world events and of civilization were to be found in the East.

From Europe, however, waves of conquest and colonization have spread to all the four corners of the earth and there is no continent today which does not bear the imprint of European influence.

This all-pervasive influence in the world's story has been secured within the last five hundred years, a period which, judged by the standards of world history, is very short. It has been won because Europe possessed a number of advantages, climatic, geographical and economic, which more than counter-balanced the political disadvantages resulting from the division of her territory between a vast number of diverse and war-like tribes. Asia bequeathed us a treasure-house rich with the offerings of a remote past; Europe's treasure-house is no less rich, but its antiquity is less. Let us take a look at some of the wonders of this masterful little continent.

First let us take Great Britain—which, comprising England, Scotland and Wales, makes up the largest of the European islands. Here was the farthest outpost of the Roman Empire, and as far as Hadrian's Great Wall, on the Scottish border, relics of its ancient Roman settlers abound. Here the Norman came and conquered, leaving behind him mighty castles, of which the Tower of London is the most famous example, and foundations of many majestic cathedrals which later blossomed into the magnificent Gothic piles we know today.

Here in lake and river valley, in sweeping downland, are the gentle charm of England's countryside, the mountain scenery of Snowdonia in Wales, and the lochs and highlands of Scotland, famed wherever beauty is cherished. Here, too, was begun that Industrial Revolution which has altered the destiny of the whole of mankind. Mighty works of engineering such as the Forth Bridge, vast shipyards on the Clyde, the Tyne and elsewhere, miracles of power plants of which Battersea Power Station is merely the most famous, of magic boxes exemplified in Broadcasting House, have arisen in every part of these islands, almost surpassing in wonder both the works of Nature and the great monuments of the past.

Scandinavia, that cluster of seafaring nations comprising Norway, Sweden, Finland and Denmark, lies just across the North Sea. Here is a land of towering mountains and vast glaciers, and far-famed fjords of exquisite beauty, of grand waterfalls harnessed for the production of " white coal " and of immense forests of conifers. One must also mention Stockholm, that royal city throned on seven islands, well called the Venice of the North and universally admired for the beauty of its Town Hall and other masterpieces of modern architecture.

CENTRAL AND WESTERN EUROPE

Germany is a country which was built up of numerous little states, each of which brought its contributions of history, art and achievement to the general pool; it is famous for the charm of its Alpine villages and the austere beauty of its riverside castles; fascinating medieval townlets in their setting of mountain, forest and defensive walls; the Hanseatic towns studding the Baltic shores; fast-growing industrial cities with their triumphs of engineering and workers' settlements, and the amazing motor roads and airports of our own day.

The Romanesque cathedrals of the Rhineland and the Gothic cathedrals of Cologne and Ulm are superb specimens of their periods. But Germany's typical architecture is rather to be found in the Renaissance of Heidelberg's Castle, the brilliant baroque architecture of Munich and Dresden, the great abbeys and bishops' palaces of Bavaria, and in the public buildings of its great cities.

Belgium and Holland, once united, have many characteristics in common. Both are small kingdoms and both are flat countries, the most densely populated of the Continent. Each is rightly proud of its ancient cities, with their relics of municipal greatness, their town halls, guildhouses and gabled mansions.

Holland is the " hollow land," the Netherlands, and its history is one of persistent struggle with the sea. The draining of the Zuider Zee is one of the world's most striking examples of human triumph over Nature.

J. Allan Cash

BEAUTY AND POWER FOR THE SERVICE OF BRITAIN'S INDUSTRY

Acclaimed as one of the most beautiful modern buildings in London, Battersea Power Station is a marvel of science housing the most up-to-date and the most powerful electricity generating plant in the country. Its total yearly output has now reached some 2,500 million units, and to produce this enormous power supply it consumes not less than 1,150,000 tons of coal a year. It was designed by Sir Giles Gilbert Scott.

France, whose long coast-line on the Atlantic and Mediterranean won her a great place in maritime commerce and a huge colonial empire, still retains a large measure of that exquisite civilization which in the latter half of the eighteenth century made her supreme in art, thought and science in all Europe. But her achievements in these fields and the vast heritage of noble buildings and works which she has bequeathed to posterity cannot hide the beauties of her fair fields. Her mountain scenery compares with any—her share of the Alps includes Europe's highest mountain, Mont Blanc—and her Mediterranean coast is world-renowned for its colourful beauty.

In architecture the greatest achievement of France is its Gothic cathedrals—Notre Dame, Chartres, Reims, Beauvais, Amiens, Rouen, Coutances, Mont St. Michel—the list could be continued almost indefinitely—and the superb chateaux of the Renaissance era.

The mountain rampart of the Pyrenees separates France from the Iberian Peninsula, five-sixths of which is Spain and one-sixth Portugal. Side by side with the monuments of a sombre Catholicism and the glorious Gothic cathedrals of Seville and Burgos, the peninsula reveals grand relics of Roman architecture, and at Granada and Cordoba souvenirs of the Moorish domination in mosques and palaces with lavishly decorated courts, halls and gardens. At its southern tip, Spain gives way to Britain in the rock-fortress of Gibraltar.

Italy is a land of romance too, by reason of its scenic charms, its radiant sunshine, the physical beauty of its people, its music and song and, above all, its visual arts, which seem to flourish here more richly than anywhere else.

ART TREASURES OF ITALY

The galleries of Europe and America are filled with Italian masterpieces without apparent diminution to the stock of art treasures in the land of their origin. What other nation can boast such a list of " art cities "? The hill towns of Bergamo and Brescia; Milan, of the white marble cathedral, and Turin, now a great manufacturing centre; Genoa, an historic seaport, with its baroque palazzi; Verona, famous for its Roman remains; Padua, famous for its ancient university and law courts; Venice, " the bride of the Adriatic," on its lagoons and canals; Mantua, Parma and Ferrara, historic centres of Renaissance art; medieval Bologna, with Europe's oldest university; the Byzantine mosaics of Ravenna; Pisa, with its cathedral, leaning tower and baptistery; Florence, the art city *par excellence*; the Umbrian hill-towns of Assisi and Perugia; Gothic Siena; the Greek temples of Paestum, and, above all, Rome, the Eternal City, with its magnificent monuments of antiquity, with Christianity's greatest church, and with the Vatican City crowning one of its seven hills. The list is well-nigh endless.

THE PLAYGROUND OF EUROPE

Across the Alpine border is Switzerland, one of the most stable and democratic countries in Europe. The peaks, passes and glaciers, the flower-decked pastures, the lakes and waterfalls of the Swiss Alps—colourful, majestic, sometimes terrific—have long been the playground of Europe. The railway tunnels which Swiss engineers have driven through some of the passes, such as the St. Gotthard, are amongst the finest wonders of modern engineering.

Austria, the westernmost of the Danubian states, too small to support its historic capital, Vienna, the second largest German-speaking city, is still one of the most beautiful provinces of the Eastern Alps, in which shelter romantic medieval villages and wonderful cities such as Salzburg and Innsbruck.

In Czechoslovakia, Prague, with its Renaissance and baroque buildings, was always a dignified and bustling city against a background of pine forests, fields and chimney-stacks, whilst Karlsbad and Marienbad, famous for their medicinal waters, are among Europe's leading spas. Hungary is a fertile plain, watered by the Danube. Budapest, a fascinating city, is the " Queen of the Danube."

A country long untouched by manufacturing activity, Yugoslavia ranges from the snow-clad Julian Alps, through the forests, mountains and waterfalls of Bosnia and Herzegovina, to one of the most entrancing coast-lines in the world—Dalmatia, with its archipelago of semi-tropical islands, and the beautiful Bay of Cattaro as the culminating point of its wonderful scenery.

There we stand at the frontier of Greece, the land in which our Western civilization had its birth. It is a wonderland of ancient beauty, for the Hellenes were a people who loved the beautiful above everything. Greece was once a nation of city states, and each of them has left us far-famed memorials of their days of glory.

D. McLeish

ST. PAUL'S—PARISH CHURCH OF BRITAIN'S METROPOLIS

Old St. Paul's was burnt down in the Great Fire, and Sir Christopher Wren designed the present cathedral, which was completed between 1675 and 1710. Its numerous tombs and monuments make it a national Temple of Fame, second only to Westminster Abbey. It is 515 feet long and 250 feet wide across the transepts; the dome is 102 feet in diameter, and the top of its cross is 336 feet 4 inches above the ground.

Even if those memorials are in ruins they are still among the supreme wonders of the world. The incomparable Parthenon, which stands among the other splendours on the Acropolis, at Athens, would alone make Greece famous. But there are also the wonders of ancient building and art to be found at Sparta, Thebes, Argos, Mycenæ and other cities.

The scenic glories of Greece lie chiefly in the Aegean Sea, studded with the far-famed isles of Greece. Chief among them, perhaps, is Crete, long, narrow and mountainous, the home of those astonishing monuments of pre-Hellenic culture known as Aegean or Minoan.

Rumania, famous alike for the magnificent scenery of the Iron Gates, where the Danube leaves the Yugoslav frontier, and for its oil-fields, among the richest in Europe, has been described as " an earthly paradise, of incalculable wealth in matters animal, vegetable and mineral."

Poland can still be proud of its ancient achievements, though many of its finest buildings were ruined during the Second World War, especially in tragic Warsaw.

Finland, or Suomi, i.e., fenland, " the land of a Thousand Lakes," presents an extraordinary sight on a large-scale map—" the land all lakes, the sea all islands." But the Finns, in their modern achievements in education and architecture—such buildings, for example, as Helsinki Railway Station—have created wonders that rival any made by nature.

RUSSIA IN EUROPE

Russia in Europe and Asia is a continent in itself, occupying nearly one-sixth of the land surface of the globe. European Russia is less than a quarter of all Russian territory, but it holds three-quarters of the population. Even to European Russia there clings the spirit of the Tartar and Mongol tribes that invaded it in the days of old. Christianity, too, here adopted a new form derived from Byzantium: its wonderful churches were crowned with bulbous domes of an Indian type and filled with jewelled ikons flickering in the incense-laden candlelight.

Side by side with the old agricultural life, in some of the world's most backward regions, there is springing up, at the bidding of intensive organization and propaganda, the full equipment of a modern industrial state: factories, built in astonishing new architectural styles, hydro-electric plants, co-operative institutions, collective farms and blocks of flats. Leningrad, once St. Petersburg, the city of the Tsars, has been supplanted as capital by Moscow, which is being completely reconstructed and even furnished with the world's most recent tube railways. Yet its Kremlin, that unique collection of palaces and cathedrals, has been preserved outwardly unchanged.

Turkey in Europe, now a minute corner of territory between the Dardanelles of tragic but glorious memory and the Black Sea, is no more than the environs of that romantic and historic city known to past ages as Byzantium or Constantinople and to us as Istanbul. Renowned alike for the beauty of its site on the famous Golden Horn, for the splendour of its mosques and for the ruins of its ancient walls, it is as rich in wonders as any corner of Europe.

MEDITERRANEAN LANDS

It is impossible to close this survey without a glance at some of those lovely islands in the blue waters of the Mediterranean.

The Balearic Islands are outposts of Spanish culture that compare with anything on the mainland. In Palma Cathedral Spanish architecture has achieved a triumph.

Next is Corsica, birthplace of Napoleon, and its neighbour Sardinia, with its prehistoric round towers and " giants' " graves.

Sicily, the largest of all the Mediterranean islands, is celebrated alike for its sulphur mines and for the architectural relics of an ancient Græco-Italian culture.

Malta, famous today as the stronghold of Britain which would not be conquered, is also celebrated for its ancient history and for the harbour fortress at Valetta, home of the Knights of St. John of Jerusalem. Rhodes, chief of the Twelve Islands, the Dodecanese, is also full of relics of those ancient and far-famed Knights Templars.

Finally, in Cyprus, the chief wonders of this British island are to be found in the grandeur of its ruined Byzantine castles and the cathedrals and monasteries.

This hasty review can serve only as an introduction to the myriad splendours, both natural and man-made, in which Europe abounds. It is in the following pages of this work, with their wealth of pictures, that a more just presentation of Europe's astonishing and impressive wealth of wonders is to be found.

E.N.A.

THE NEW "OLD LADY OF THREADNEEDLE STREET"

The financial centre of London, a leading money market of the world, is the Bank of England, founded in 1694. It stands in the heart of the city close to the Royal Exchange, and this view of the main entrance shows the new superstructure. A guard, provided by the War Office, is always stationed in the Bank.

Mondiale

LONDON'S GRIM AND ANCIENT FORTRESS

This view of the Tower of London shows clearly the two lines of fortifications around the Keep or White Tower, begun by William the Conqueror about 1078. Most of the existing fortress was completed before the thirteenth century. In the Wakefield Tower, one of the thirteen towers on the inner wall, are kept the Crown Jewels. The two towers seen in the inner wall in this picture are the Lanthorn Tower and the Salt Tower.

D. McLeish

NERVE CENTRE OF BRITISH BROADCASTING

Broadcasting House, in Portland Place, is one of modern London's most spectacular buildings, if only for the striking symmetry of its design. Here are the chief offices and studios of the British Broadcasting Corporation and a veritable magician's box of intricate machinery and delicate apparatus. The sculptured figures of Prospero and Ariel which may be seen above the entrance were designed by Eric Gill.

Aerofilms Ltd.

MYSTERIOUS MONUMENT OF PREHISTORIC BRITAIN

Stonehenge, the group of huge stones on Salisbury Plain, was erected either as a Sun Temple or as a sepulchre about 1700 B.C. Sixteen of the thirty stones in the outer circle still stand and average $13\frac{1}{2}$ feet in height and 26 tons in weight. How such stones were erected without machinery remains a mystery.

D. McLeish

ENGLAND'S ROMAN BULWARK

Hadrian's Wall, the most impressive Roman monument in Britain, was built about A.D. 120 by order of the Emperor Hadrian, and was held by Roman troops until late in the fourth century A.D. It ran for 75 miles from Bowness, on the Solway Firth, to Wallsend, near the mouth of the Tyne, and its course can still be traced in its entirety. This finely preserved section is 8 feet thick and over 6 feet in height.

Royal Commission on Hist. Monuments, by permission of the Controller, H.M.S.O.

HENRY VII's CHAPEL—WESTMINSTER ABBEY

Built between 1503 and 1519, Henry VII's Chapel, which forms the eastern end of Westminster Abbey, is recognized as the supreme example of Tudor Gothic in all Britain. The elaborate beauty of its sculptured detail, and particularly of the superb fan-tracery roof with its carved stone pendants, is one of England's architectural glories. The stalls and banners hung along the sides are those of the Knights of the Bath.

Photochrom

G. E. Abraham

LARGEST CATHEDRAL IN BRITAIN

York Minster was founded as a Benedictine abbey in 1093 and most of the original Norman work remains. The West Front is a superb example of fourteenth-century decorated Gothic style. In the left of its twin towers, 196 feet high, hangs the 11-ton bell, Big Peter, struck at noon. The central tower is 198 feet high.

THE MAJESTY OF SNOWDON

Snowdon, 3,560 feet high and the highest mountain in Great Britain south of the Scottish border, lies in the north-west corner of Wales. The highest peak is known to the Welsh as "y Wyddfa," and is renowned as one of the most beautiful peaks in the world. This view shows the famous "horseshoe" below the summit. The railway to the summit travels up the northern, and less precipitous, side.

E.N.A.

STEEL SPANS ACROSS THE FIRTH OF FORTH

The magnificent cantilever bridge which carries the railway across the Firth of Forth, Scotland, was opened in 1890, and was acclaimed as the greatest engineering triumph of its age. It measures over a mile and a half in length, including approaches. The huge steel towers reach a height of 360 feet.

Sport and General

THE *QUEEN MARY* LEAVES THE CLYDE SHIPYARDS

One of the largest, and certainly the finest, group of shipyards in the world is to be found on the Clyde below Glasgow. Here has been built one famous ship after another, and this picture shows the Cunard-White Star liner *Queen Mary* leaving her dock in John Brown & Co.'s yards after her completion.

Mondiale *R. Adam*

GLENCOE, SCENE OF A NOTORIOUS MASSACRE

Scotland is famous for the almost unparalleled beauty of its wild mountains, lochs and glens; none of these last is more historic, even if a few are more exquisite, than Glencoe, where the Macdonald clansmen were massacred by the Campbells on the questionable order of William III in 1692. Here is Glencoe flanked by mist-wreathed peaks, as seen from Loch Leven's far shore.

ST. KEVIN'S TOWER

The Vale of Glendalough, County Wicklow, in Eire, is celebrated for its remains of the monastery founded there early in the sixth century by St. Kevin, the hermit. This view of the ruins shows in the foreground the famous Round Tower, a type of structure characteristic of primitive Irish Christianity. The tower is 110 feet high and only 52 feet in circumference. The conical cap is a reconstruction from some of the original stones.

E.N.A.

A FANTASY OF NATURE

Nature wrought strangely in fashioning the caves on the Island of Staffa (i.e., Pillar Island), off the coast of Argyllshire. Of volcanic origin, they are formed from huge hexagonal pillars of basalt for all the world like man-made columns. Fingal's Cave, shown here, named after the half-mythical Scottish hero, is the largest and finest; it measures 227 feet in length, and at its maximum is some 60 feet in height.

E.N.A.

VAST STONES OF THE GIANT'S CAUSEWAY

Here is another example of volcanic action producing remarkable columns of basalt. The Giant's Causeway, a promontory on the coast of Co. Antrim, Northern Ireland, is, like Fingal's Cave, the result of volcanic action, and part of the same system. Some of the stone pillars are as much as 60 feet in height.

Nordisk Pressefoto

LINKING JUTLAND WITH THE ISLAND OF FUNEN

The channel known as the Little Belt separates the mainland of Denmark (Jutland) from the Island of Funen and imposes serious restrictions on communications. These were overcome when, between 1929 and 1934, Danish engineers constructed this superb railway bridge. It is 1,285 yards long and 100 feet high.

E.N.A.

HAMLET'S CASTLE

If it were famous for nothing else, the royal castle of Kronborg would be remembered as the scene of "Hamlet". It lies in the town of Helsingör, Shakespeare's Elsinore. Actually it is a magnificent example of the Dutch Renaissance style, dating back to 1577. Today it is used principally as a maritime museum.

Moholy-Nagy

SUNSHINE AND SHADOWS AT MIDNIGHT

Amongst the most interesting of natural phenomena is that known as the Midnight Sun. In far northern latitudes the sun never sinks below the horizon during June and July and daylight continues for weeks on end. This interesting picture was taken at midnight at Tromsö, on the north-west coast of Norway.

Lubinski

WHITE COAL

The River Göta, in the south of Sweden, descends 108 feet in under a mile, thereby forming the six imposing Trollhättan Falls, besides several rapids. Their water-power is utilised by a number of factories, and more especially by a triumph of engineering in the form of the Trollhättan Power Station, the greatest in Sweden, with turbines which can generate up to 166,000 h.p.

SWEDEN'S OLDEST CATHEDRAL

Founded about the year 1080 by St. Knut, King of Denmark, Lund Cathedral is the oldest and most important Romanesque building in Sweden. The existing structure dates entirely from the twelfth century and is free from subsequent additions of consequence. The magnificent crypt under the choir and transepts is a celebrated feature of the edifice.

E.N.A.

Gunnar Lundh

E.N.A.

CLOVERLEAF TRAFFIC CROSSING

The problem of dealing with heavy cross-traffic in the confines of a busy city has been solved in Stockholm by a cross-over combining grace with efficiency. Here is the famous "cloverleaf" road junction on the busy Slussen thoroughfare, which, while providing an uninterrupted route in any desired direction, obviates any stoppages in the steady flow of traffic.

EUROPE'S QUAINTEST CHURCH

The Habokyrka, in the south Swedish province of Skaraborg, not far from Jönköping, is one of the most remarkable of the ancient timber churches for which Sweden is renowned. Its wooden walls and ceiling are entirely covered with paintings illustrating sacred subjects. These, in the olden days, formed the Bible of those who could not read. The church is extremely old, but was partly rebuilt in 1723.

VENERABLE GOTHIC FANE IN OLD UTRECHT

St. Willibrord, the Apostle of the Frisians, founded Utrecht Cathedral, a magnificent specimen of thirteenth-century Gothic architecture. The belfry, detached from the rest of the building, houses forty-two bells (one of which weighs 8½ tons); it rises to a height of 338 feet, and to enjoy the magnificent view from the top, the visitor must climb 458 steps.

THE RECLAMATION OF THE ZUIDER ZEE

One of the greatest engineering works of modern times is the reclamation of the Zuider Zee, which, when finished, will add over 800 square miles to Holland's territory. Here is a view, taken before the German occupation, of the main embankment, 18 miles long, showing some of the thirty discharge sluice gates, each 33 feet wide and having a depth of 16½ feet.

Topical

D. McLeish

UNIQUE RELIC OF MEDIEVAL GERMANY

For centuries the small Bavarian town of Rothenburg lay forgotten behind dense beech forests. Today it is probably unique as an unspoiled medieval survival. Above is shown the White Tower, an original part of the wall pulled down in the thirteenth century. The later wall is still in good repair.

Ullstein

GEMS OF MEDIEVAL SCULPTURE IN NUREMBERG'S MARKET-PLACE

The " Beautiful Fountain " with its wealth of statuary, set amid the crowded stalls of Nuremberg market-place, dates from 1385 and is 60 feet in height. On the left stands Our Lady's Church, famous for its two-storied porch and for its quaint clock-figures of the Electors that walk in procession daily at noon. The fountain survived the widespread havoc caused by Allied air raids during the Second World War.

Keystone

THE BLACK GATE, RELIC OF ROMAN CONQUEST

The North Gate of the city of Treves (Trier), called Porta Nigra or the Black Gate from its smoke-blackened condition, is one of the greatest Roman monuments north of the Alps. The city was founded by the Emperor Augustus, and the gate erected about the third century. For six centuries it was used as a church.

D. McLeish

SANS SOUCI, FREDERICK THE GREAT'S LOVELY RETREAT

Built in 1745–1747 with his own money and from his own design, Sans Souci at Potsdam was Frederick the Great's beloved retreat from state cares. The Prussian monarch expressed an unfulfilled wish to be buried on its terrace: "*Quand je serai là, je serai sans souci*" (When I am there, I shall be free from care). He died here in 1786, and his apartments were preserved exactly as they were in his day.

E. O. Hoppé

HEIDELBERG'S ROSE-RED PALACE

Heidelberg Castle, the palace of the Electors Palatine, was burnt by the French in 1693 and, though repaired, it was ruined by lightning in 1764. Its inner courtyard is one of the most picturesque sights in Germany, with its charming red sandstone façades of the sixteenth and seventeenth centuries. Nowadays it remains a rare haven of peace amid the devastation left in the wake of the Second World War.

Paul Popper

ANGULAR ARCHITECTURE FOR MODERN OFFICES

Among the cities of Germany, Hamburg, before the Second World War, had acquired an outstanding reputation for the beauty of its modern as well as its ancient buildings. The Burchard-Strasse, in particular, was lined with great office-blocks, of which the chief survivor is the Chile House, a ten-storied structure completed in 1924 after four years' labour. Its angular architecture is shown clearly in the photograph.

E.N.A.

MEDIEVAL GRANDEUR OF BRUSSELS TOWN HALL

The fifteenth-century Hôtel de Ville of Brussels is perhaps Belgium's most historic building. It is on the fourth side of the Grand Place, one of the most beautiful public squares in Europe, the other three sides of which are formed by other notable buildings, including the intricately decorated Maison du Roi. The superbly carved spire, 360 feet high, is crowned by a gilded figure of St. Michael, the city's patron.

Sport and General

MALINES AND ITS MIGHTY CATHEDRAL

Malines' grand Gothic Cathedral is notable for its colossal tower, which is over 300 feet in height and would have been the highest in Christendom had the builders' original intention been carried out. Malines, or Mechlin, famous in the Middle Ages for its lace, is the seat of the Archbishop Primate of Belgium.

E. O. Hoppé

THE RESURRECTION OF YPRES

Ypres was reduced to a mass of rubble during the First World War. Phoenix-like, it rose again from its ashes, and the incomparable Cloth Hall and the Cathedral were built anew, faithfully to the original lines. As a memorial to this first wholesale aggression, part of the ruins were left undisturbed.

Photos: Lubinski

PLACID BEAUTY OF GHENT'S MOST FAMOUS CANAL

Belgium's intricate network of canals, like that of the Netherlands, forms one of the country's chief means of communication. Here is the famous Canal de la Lys at Ghent, with the crow-step gables of its ancient guildhouses mirrored in the placid waterway and, in the distance, one of 200 bridges and the fifteenth-century church of St. Michael.

AN ANCIENT BELGIAN BELFRY

The old Market Hall in the main square of Bruges is dwarfed by its stupendous and still older Belfry, which rises above the rest of the building to a height of 260 feet. The Belfry houses the carillon of forty-nine bells, celebrated not only for the sweetness of their tone but also for the fact that, until the outbreak of the First World War, they had been rung daily since the early sixteenth century.

Fox

THE EIFFEL TOWER, EUROPE'S TALLEST STRUCTURE

Erected by an engineer named Gustave Eiffel for the Paris Exhibition of 1889, the Eiffel Tower, 984 feet in height, was the world's tallest structure until the completion of the Empire State Building in New York, and is still the tallest in Europe. The panoramic view from the top extends over a radius of sixty miles.

E.N.A.

THE HEART OF MODERN PARIS

The Place de la Concorde is by many people considered to be the most beautiful square in the world. The obelisk in the centre was presented to Louis-Philippe and brought from Luxor in Egypt, and occupies the approximate site of the guillotine on which Louis XVI, Marie Antoinette and nearly three thousand other victims of the Revolutionary Terror met their fate. In the background may be seen the basilica of Sacré Cœur.

D. McLeish

THE MADELEINE, WHERE PARISIAN FASHION WORSHIPS

In the heart of fashionable Paris stands La Madeleine, the beautiful Church of St. Mary Magdalene. It was designed by Pierre Vignon in 1804 by order of Napoleon, who intended it as a temple of glory, and its strikingly simple lines follow those of a Roman temple. The pediment sculpture depicts the Last Judgment.

E.N.A.

VERSAILLES, MIGHTY PALACE OF " LE ROI SOLEIL "

Most of the Palace of Versailles, the largest in the world, was built by Louis XIV, known from his passion for display as " Le Roi Soleil." Over 30,000 men laboured on it for some thirty years at a cost of 500 million francs. The main building once housed 10,000 persons. In the courtyard stands Louis XIV's statue.

E.N.A.

SWEEPING VISTAS IN THE GARDENS OF VERSAILLES

The Park and Gardens of Versailles, designed by André le Nôtre and adorned with a multitude of fountains and statues, are unrivalled of their kind. This view from the terrace gives an idea of their enormous extent. It shows the main avenue with the Basin of Latona in the foreground, the stretch of the " Green Carpet " and the Grand Canal beyond. This canal is a mile long and some 200 feet in width.

D. McLeish

MASSIVE TOWERS OF CARCASSONNE

Unique among Europe's remaining medieval fortresses is Carcassonne. Its foundations date from the times of the Romans and Visigoths. Later additions belong to many periods, mainly the eleventh and twelfth centuries. From 1849 to 1879 the entire system was carefully and authentically restored by Viollet-le-Duc, the most prominent architect of the Gothic revival in France. The work was completed after his death.

E.N.A.

GRACE AND BEAUTY OF CHARTRES CATHEDRAL

None of the Gothic cathedrals for which France is so famous has greater claims to distinction than Chartres, whose towers dominate the wide plains of Beauce. Built between 1194 and 1240, it is the third on the site, and is famed on three counts: in the graceful statuary of its portals, in the marvellous colouring of its ancient stained glass and in the majesty of its north-west spire, 377 feet high. The shorter spire measures 351 feet.

D. McLeish

MYSTERIOUS MONUMENTS IN OLD BRITTANY

Set up on the coast of Brittany three to four thousand years ago lies the greatest collection of megalithic monuments in the world. Of these the most spectacular are the "Alignments," of which there are several distinct sets. The picture shows those of Kermario (i.e., Place of the Dead), consisting of ten rows some 1,300 yards in length, comprising 982 granite stones or menhirs, some of which are over 18 feet high and weigh as much as 50 tons each. Many stones from this site have been used for road-mending.

D. McLeish

A BRIDGE NEARLY TWO THOUSAND YEARS OLD

This remaining portion of the Pont du Gard, near Nîmes, is 295 yards long and 160 feet high. Said to date from 19 B.C., when it was constructed as an aqueduct to bring water from a source 25 miles distant, it is one of the most famous extant examples of the durability of the old Roman masonry.

E.N.A.

MONT ST. MICHEL, FAMOUS GOTHIC JEWEL

On the summit of a granite islet a mile off the coast near Pontorson, La Manche, is the historic abbey-fortress of Mont St. Michel, founded in the eighth century A.D., although most of it is considerably later, and today it is reckoned as a famous survival of Gothic architecture. During the Hundred Years War it successfully resisted several sieges by the English. Isolated at high tide, it is united to the mainland by a causeway.

E.N.A.

THE CORNICHE, THE RIVIERA'S GREAT ROAD

The Corniche, that marvellous military road built by Napoleon between Nice and Genoa, is cut into the precipitous cliffs of the Maritime Alps overhanging the Mediterranean. Today few more famous motor roads exist in Europe, for the scenery is superb. Here is the road passing the castle-crowned rock of Eze.

E.N.A.

ORNATE ARCHITECTURE OF A FAMOUS SPANISH CATHEDRAL

Burgos Cathedral was founded in 1221 by the sainted King Ferdinand III. Built of white limestone, mainly by French and German architects, it was not completed until 1567. Its layout resembles that of a French cathedral, but the lavish decoration is typical of Spanish architecture. The eight-sided central tower and the openwork of the west towers are marvels of the " plateresque " style of the 16th century.

E.N.A.

REVOLUTIONARY ARCHITECTURE IN CATALONIA'S CAPITAL

The Casa Mila y Campo, in the Barcelona avenue called Paseo de Gracia, is one of the strangest blocks of modern flats in Europe. It is a striking example of the Catalan architect Gaudi's *art nouveau* designs, all curves and no corners. Note especially the intriguing balconies and the curious chimney-stacks.

E.N.A.

SPANISH ROYALTY'S FORMER HOME

The Royal Palace at Madrid, whose last occupants were King Alfonso XIII and Queen Ena, was built in 1738-1764 for King Philip V. It is a huge seven-storied structure of the Corinthian order, and covers nearly six acres, being 470 feet square and 100 feet in height. The building material is white granite. The Royal Library and one of the most celebrated collections of old armour and tapestry are housed here.

E.N.A.

ANCIENT ABBEY IN A CATALAN FASTNESS

Nearly 3,000 feet above sea-level and perched on a terrace amongst the fantastic saw-edges of the Montserrat Mountains stands the ancient Abbey, famous throughout Christendom for its possession of a Holy Image of the Virgin, reputed to have been carved by St. Luke and brought to Spain by St. Peter. It is a small, black wooden carving, but of world-wide fame, and attracts some 60,000 pilgrims yearly.

Paul Popper

THE ALHAMBRA, MASTERPIECE OF MOORISH ART

Picturesquely set on the hills near Granada, in southern Spain, this ancient fortress-palace was erected by the Moors in the 13th and 14th centuries. Its peerless decorations, largely by unknown artists, were in great part spoiled after the expulsion of the Moors in 1482, but it remains a treasure-house of art.

E.N.A.

THE MONASTERY-PALACE OF THE ESCORIAL

Built in 1563–1595 by Philip II, Queen Mary of England's husband, the Escorial almost rivals Versailles for size and grandeur among the royal palaces of Europe. Nearly 230 yards long and 180 yards wide, it has 16 courts, 2,673 windows, 86 staircases and 100 miles of corridors. The buildings, which lie some miles to the north-west of Madrid, include a famous monastery, a great church and the royal burial vault.

E.N.A.

AVILA, RELIC OF MEDIEVAL SPAIN

Situated on a stony table-land, 3,650 feet above sea-level, Avila is the outstanding example of a medieval walled town. Its perfect girdle of ramparts, a mile and a half in circuit, with eight gates and eighty semi-circular towers, was reconstructed by King Alfonso VI of Castile for protection against the Moors.

E.N.A.

CORDOBA'S WONDERFUL MOSQUE-CATHEDRAL

The celebrated Mosque of Cordoba, now a cathedral, is one of the finest relics of the Moorish occupation of Spain, which lasted from A.D. 711 to 1492. One of the largest mosques in Western Islam, it covers an area of over 27,000 square yards, and this picture shows some of the 856 pillars of jasper, porphyry and multi-coloured marble, every one differently carved and decorated, that support the characteristic arches of the roof.

E.N.A.

FAIRY PALACE OF THE MOORISH KINGS

The famous Alhambra Palace at Granada is claimed to be the crowning achievement of the Moors in Spain. No part of it is more wonderful than the Court of Lions, which derives its name from the marble figures by its fountain. The walls and arches are decorated with exquisite arabesques like ivory carving.

E.N.A.

HUGE ARCHES OF PORTUGAL'S GREATEST AQUEDUCT

The magnificent Aqueduct of the Aguas Livres carries Lisbon's chief water supply from a brook near the village of Bellas, some 15 miles away. It was built between 1729 and 1749, and the engineering skill and beauty in its design are best revealed in this section, where the water is conveyed across the valley of the small River Alcantara by a structure of thirty-five arches, many of which exceed 200 feet in height.

E. O. Hoppé

THE HOUSE OF THE POINTS

One of the strangest houses in the world is the Casa dos Bicos or "House of the Points," in the Rua dos Bacalhoeiros, Lisbon. It was built four hundred years ago by the son of a rich nobleman and was popularly supposed to have a diamond concealed in each point. Many were, in consequence, broken off.

E. O. Hoppé

SUNLIT SPLENDOUR OF BELEM'S CLOISTERS

In Belem (that is, Bethlehem), a suburb of Lisbon, is the wonderful old Hieronymite monastery founded in 1499. A masterpiece in white limestone, of the style of architecture known as Manueline, it is distinguished chiefly by its cloisters (seen here). Neither their candelabra-like columns, every inch of which is decorated with delicate carving, nor their groined vaulting have needed restoration since they were built.

E.N.A.

TWELFTH-CENTURY CASTLE-CHURCH OF OLD PORTUGAL

The older of Coimbra's two cathedrals is this strange building. A splendid example of the Romanesque style, it dates from the twelfth century and incorporates parts of the older Moorish mosque on the site of which it grew up. The military needs of Portugal's early history are clearly shown in its design, for the church had, on many occasions, to serve as a fortress. Note the charming stone fountain beneath it.

E.N.A.

STRANGE CHIMNEYS OF CINTRA'S PALACE

The Royal Palace of Cintra, built during the fourteenth and fifteenth centuries, partly in the Moorish style, is celebrated for its two immense conical chimneys which carried off the smoke from the vast kitchens. For many years it was the summer resort of the royal family, for the beauties of Cintra are world-famous, and have frequently been sung by poets, including the English Lord Byron in his *Childe Harold.*

E.N.A.

THE STELVIO, ONE OF EUROPE'S HIGHEST ROADS

The road through the Italian Alps from Merano to Bormio attains a height of 9,049 feet at the top of the Stelvio Pass and is clear of snow only from midsummer to mid-October. The picture shows the descent to Trafoi, 4,000 feet below. The zigzags are so sharp that some vehicles have to reverse at every bend.

D. McLeish

THE COLOSSEUM, SYMBOL OF ROME'S GREATNESS

The Colosseum, one of the world's most stupendous structures, although two-thirds of its original masonry has disappeared, was completed in A.D. 80. It measured nearly one-third of a mile in circumference and 160 feet in height, and it seated over 50,000 spectators. Gladiatorial contests, wild beast fights and naval contests were staged in this amphitheatre, and countless Christian martyrs were here thrown to the lions.

Lubinski

ST. PETER'S, CHRISTENDOM'S GREATEST CHURCH

The Basilica of St. Peter, within the Vatican City, was founded by the Emperor Constantine over the saint's grave and rebuilt between 1506 and 1626. Its dimensions are truly titanic: length 694 feet, width 375 feet, area 163,000 square feet. Michelangelo's incomparable dome is 436 feet high and 139 feet in span.

THE CIVIC CENTRE

The nerve centre of Rome's world-wide empire was the Forum, this view of which is taken from the Palatine Hill. The three columns in the foreground belonged to the famous Temple of Castor and Pollux, and in the exact centre of the picture, beyond the Sacred Way, is the Triumphal Arch of the Emperor Septimius

D. McLeish

ᶠ ANCIENT ROME
verus. The group of columns to the left of this are relics of the Temple of Concord and that of the
nperor Vespasian. The building in front of the domed church was once the Curia or Senate House. In
e background rises the enormous National Monument in white marble to King Victor Emmanuel II.

Mondiale

THE FRESCO MASTERPIECES OF THE SISTINE CHAPEL

The papal chapel in the Vatican was built for Sixtus IV in 1473–1481 and is adorned with what are generally considered the world's finest frescoes. The side-walls were painted by the most celebrated Florentine artists of the period, but their work is completely outshone by Michelangelo's ceiling and altar-wall, and the latter in particular, depicting the Last Judgment, is one of the most glorious creations of human genius.

Mondiale

CONSTANTINE'S ARCH—THE TRIUMPH OF CHRISTIANITY

The Arch of Constantine, adjoining the Colosseum, was erected in honour of the first Christian emperor's victory (under the Sign of the Cross) over his pagan rival Maxentius, A.D. 312. It is the best-preserved, best-proportioned triumphal arch in Rome, but most of the decorations came from earlier structures.

E.N.A.

THE ANCIENT BRIDGE OF FLORENCE

The Ponte Vecchio, or Old Bridge, over the River Arno at Florence, is one of the most famous and picturesque bridges in the world. Erected in its present form in the year 1345, after previous reconstructions, it is lined with goldsmiths' shops, which are built into the arches and overhang the river. In 1944 the retreating German forces destroyed buildings at either end, but left the historic structure undamaged.

Mondiale

LEANING TOWER OF PISA IN ITS HARMONIOUS SETTING

Pisa's group of ecclesiastical buildings in white marble, dating in the main from the twelfth century, are unparalleled for their harmonious beauty—Baptistry, Cathedral and the six-hundred-year-old Campanile or Leaning Tower, which is 179 feet high and, on account of subsidence, 14 feet out of the perpendicular.

Lubinski

THE GLORIOUS SWEEP OF NAPLES BAY

Europe has no fairer scene than the Bay of Naples, the exquisite curve of which is displayed to perfection in this view from the heights of Posillipo. The terraced houses of Italy's third city rise in a great amphitheatre from the azure sea, and in the dim distance is Vesuvius, with its eternal plume of smoke. The Bay itself, with its vast expanse of smooth water, is a favourite resort for pleasure craft.

D. McLeish

THE WONDERFUL DOME AND TOWER OF FLORENCE CATHEDRAL

Florence's Cathedral, dating from the fourteenth century and faced with coloured marble, has three features of consummate architectural merit—Brunelleschi's marvellous dome, 351 feet high, the first in which a double skin was used; Giotto's campanile, 275 feet high; and, near it, the Baptistry (a corner of which is seen on the right of this picture), an octagonal building with Ghiberti's world-famous bronze doors.

D. McLeish

MILAN CATHEDRAL'S CROWDED SPIRES AND PINNACLES

Milan Cathedral, after St. Peter's, Rome, is the largest church in Italy. Built entirely of white marble, it was begun in 1386 but not completed until 1805. Its length is 486 feet, width 289 feet, and the statue of the Virgin on the central tower is 354 feet above the ground. The roof is adorned with 135 pinnacles.

Sport and General

THE ORIENTAL SPLENDOUR OF ST. MARK'S

St. Mark's Basilica, Venice, was founded for the reception of the bones of St. Mark, brought from Alexandria, A.D. 829. Its semi-Byzantine architecture, with over five hundred marble columns and priceless mosaics, is unique in Western Europe. Pigeons have thronged its piazza from time immemorial.

E.N.A.

ONCE HEADQUARTERS OF THE VENETIAN REPUBLIC

The Doges' Palace, with its lovely loggias, is the classic example of Venetian Gothic architecture. On the left are the two tall columns erected in 1180 in the Piazzetta, one of which is crowned with the winged Lion of St. Mark, the other with a statue of St. Theodore. Beyond them stands the famous Old Library.

D. McLeish

MAIN ARTERY OF THE CITY OF CANALS

Venice is the city of canals, bridges and romantic gondolas. The Grand Canal, lined with the old palaces of its merchant-princes and spanned in a single 90-foot leap by the famous Rialto Bridge, a marble structure of 1592, is the city's chief highway. The gondola posts are painted in their owners' colours.

Lubinski

PAESTUM'S GREEK TEMPLE ON ITALIAN SOIL

The ancient Greek city of Paestum, or Poseidonia, in Lucania, is celebrated for its three temples, of which the noblest is the Temple of Poseidon (Neptune). With its thirty-six Doric columns of yellow travertine, it is a marvellously preserved survival from the sixth century B.C., that golden age of Hellenic architecture.

F. Henle

AMAZING PRESERVATION OF ROMAN POMPEII

The eruption of Mount Vesuvius, A.D. 79, covered the ancient Roman towns of Herculaneum and Pompeii with layers of ashes and mud to a depth of 20–100 feet. Their ruins were thus preserved for centuries, awaiting only skilful excavation and restoration. This picture shows the remains of the Temple of Jupiter and a triumphal arch at Pompeii, with the smoking cone of Mount Vesuvius in the background. The Temple of Jupiter and other ancient monuments suffered damage when Pompeii was bombed in 1943.

E. Meerkamper

THE MATTERHORN—EUROPE'S MOST THEATRICAL MOUNTAIN

The Matterhorn's isolated obelisk soars to a height of 14,780 feet from the Alpine glaciers on the Swiss–Italian frontier. Here it is seen mirrored in the waters of the Schwarzsee, near Zermatt. The summit was first reached on July 14, 1865, by Edward Whymper's party, four of whom lost their lives on the descent.

Swiss Federal Railways

THE ONE-TIME HEADQUARTERS OF THE OLD LEAGUE OF NATIONS

The vast headquarters of the old League of Nations, comparable in size with the Palace of Versailles, overlooks Lake Geneva and covers an area of nearly 5 acres. Built between 1931 and 1937 at a cost of a million pounds, it housed the Assembly Hall, Council Room, Library and Secretariat of the League.

E.N.A.

THE ST. GOTTHARD TUNNEL, MARVEL OF RAILWAY ENGINEERING

The St. Gotthard Railway, built between 1872 and 1882 at a cost of £12,000,000, is the boldest in Europe. Near Giornico, for instance, the engineers were faced with a sudden 700-foot drop. They solved the problem by means of two spiral tunnels, and at one point, as seen here, there are three lines one above the other.

Swiss Federal Railways

D. McLeish

A TRAVELLERS' AID—THE ST. BERNARD HOSPICE

The Hospice of the Great St. Bernard, on the Swiss–Italian frontier, was founded in 1045 for the purpose of providing shelter and food for travellers. At 8,114 feet this is the highest dwelling in Europe. Here are kept the famous St. Bernard dogs which help the monks to track travellers lost in the snows of the St. Bernard Pass.

EARTH PILLARS—A FREAK OF NATURE

The Val d'Hérens, a lateral valley of the Rhône in the Valais canton, has a strange sight to show. Moraine deposits of the Ice Age, composed of soft rock and soil, have been denuded by rain action in such a fashion as to produce earth-pillars, some of which are capped with large stones.

Kondor Pressedienst M. Schur

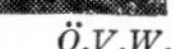

Ö.V.W.

THE MAGNIFICENT GLOCKNER ROAD

The Glocknerstrasse crosses the Hohe Tauern range in the vicinity of the Grossglockner, Austria's highest mountain. Over 16 miles long, it has a uniform width of 20 feet and an average gradient of 1 in 8, and ascends to a height of 8,225 feet above sea-level. It was constructed as a toll-road by a syndicate, 1931–35.

MELK ABBEY

The Benedictine Abbey of Melk, proudly throned on the bank of the Danube, is one of the most magnificent specimens of Baroque architecture in existence. Founded in 1089, it was entirely rebuilt between 1700 and 1750. The building itself is 400 yards long. The picture shows the west front, with the ornate twin towers and dome of the church.

Courtesy of Austrian Legation

A BAROQUE MASTERPIECE

The Karlskirche, seen above, was dedicated by the Emperor Charles VI to St. Charles Borromeo after the cessation of a devasting plague in 1713. Designed by Fischer von Erlach, it is the most important baroque church in Vienna. Building was begun in 1715, but the structure was not completed until 1737. Although seven bombs fell near it during the 1939–45 War, it suffered very little damage.

Robert Byron

OLDEST SYNAGOGUE IN EUROPE

The oldest synagogue in Prague, and probably in Europe, is the Staronová Synagogă, in the Joseph-town quarter. The Jews have been settled in Prague since the eleventh century, and this synagogue was rebuilt in early Gothic style after the Ghetto was burned down in 1338.

THE WONDERFUL ICE CAVERN OF DOBŠIŇA

Not far from Dobšińa, a small mining town situated in the middle of the limestone Carpathian Mountains, is the largest ice cavern in Europe. It contains an icefield which covers a total area of some 10,000 square yards, and many of its ice formations are of startling dimensions and possess a fantastic beauty.

E.N.A.

Centropress

THE HISTORIC BRIDGE, CASTLE AND CATHEDRAL OF PRAGUE

The Charles Bridge over the River Vltava at Prague, with its sixteen arches, its twenty-eight statues and its Gothic gate-towers, is 550 yards in length and undoubtedly one of the world's finest bridges. In the distance, the Hradčany hill dominates the city with its immense fortified palace (once the headquarters of the Czechoslovak Government and the residence of the President) and its cathedral of St. Vitus.

Dorien Leigh

WHERE THE HUNGARIAN KINGS WERE CROWNED

Begun in the Romanesque period, 1255–1269, the magnificent Coronation Church at Budapest was gothicized in the next century. The right-hand tower, 260 feet high, was erected under King Matthias Corvinus; that on the left by the founder of the church, Belá IV. In front is a column to the Holy Trinity. During the Turkish occupation of the city it was used as a mosque. It was completely restored, 1873–1896.

Magyar Köyponti Hiradó

EUROPE'S GREATEST PARLIAMENT HOUSE

Budapest boasts the greatest Parliament House in Europe, a vast limestone building in late Gothic style, covering an area of $4\frac{1}{3}$ acres. Begun in 1885 and completed 21 years later, it is 870 feet long, and its dome is 315 feet high. The exterior statues are of Hungarian Kings, statesmen and generals.

P. Morton Shand

ZAGREB'S UP-TO-DATE SCHOOL

Zagreb, or Agram, is the second city of Yugoslavia and the capital of Croatia. One is accustomed to think of the Yugoslavs as a purely agricultural and somewhat backward nation, but this picture of one of Zagreb's ultra-modern schools shows that in respect of educational architecture they are conversant with the latest achievements. The building is designed to admit the maximum sunlight into every room.

E.N.A.

THE CETINJE ROAD—A TRIUMPH OF ROAD BUILDING

The zigzag highway from Cattaro to Cetinje, a distance of 38 miles, was built by the Austrians in 1876–1881. It crosses the Bukovica Pass, 4,090 feet above sea-level, and overlooks some of the most impressive scenery in Europe. The picture shows the zigzags on the slope of Mount Lovćen (5,771 feet).

Lubinski

DIOCLETIAN'S SUPERB PALACE AT SPLIT

Split (Spalato) possesses the Palace of the Emperor Diocletian, who in this lovely spot built himself a sumptuous place of retirement, where he died A.D. 313. The Palace fell into ruins after the Emperor's death, but in A.D. 639 invasion by the Alvars of the nearby city of Salona caused the inhabitants to seek refuge within its massive walls. They later obtained permission from the Court of Constantinople to make their homes here, and in A.D. 659 a bishopric was created in the newly named city of Spalato. This was the beginning of the modern town.

N. Zographos

TEMPLE OF ERECHTHEUS, TWO THOUSAND THREE HUNDRED YEARS OLD

The Erechtheum, or Temple of Erechtheus, the legendary founder of Athens, was completed in 407 B.C. and is the premier example of Ionic art, of exquisite perfection of detail. The Portico of the Caryatides, in particular, with its roof supported by six figures of maidens, is an architectural jewel beyond price.

N. Zographos

THE SOUL-STIRRING BEAUTY OF THE PARTHENON

By universal consent the Parthenon is the supreme example of antique art. Perfect in proportion and detail, and built entirely of Pentelic marble, this marvellous structure was completed in ten years (447–438 B.C.). It had ninety-eight fluted Doric columns, a bas-relief frieze 524 feet long, ninety-two sculptured metopes, and a 42-feet high ivory statue of Athena, patron goddess of the city of Athens. During the fighting in December 1944, the cornice and some columns and steps were very slightly damaged.

THE STATELY ACROPOLIS—HALLOWED

Dominating Athens from the south rises the Acropolis, a steep limestone plateau, 512 feet above sea-level. Site of the earliest settlement, then a citadel, under Pericles, it was devoted entirely to the worship of the gods. The temples that were then erected, though now partly in ruins, provide the best extant picture

N. Zographos

CENTRE OF ANCIENT ATHENS

of the supreme Hellenic arts of architecture and sculpture. On the sky-line, from left to right in this picture, are the Propylæa or gatehouse, the Erechtheum and the incomparable Parthenon. At the foot of the rock is the graceful Colonnade of Eumenes, which connected the Odeon with the Theatre of Dionysos.

Lubinski

THE NATIONAL THEATRE OF ANCIENT ATHENS

The plays of Aeschylus, Sophocles, Euripides and Aristophanes received their first performances at the open-air Theatre of Dionysos, the present arrangements of which date from Roman times. Hollowed out of the south slopes of the Acropolis, it is of semicircular shape, with a radius of 165 feet; it accommodated an audience of 17,000. The actors performed on the paved courtyard in the centre.

E.N.A.

FAITHFUL RECONSTRUCTION OF THE WORLD'S MOST FAMOUS STADIUM

Constructed in 330 B.C., the Stadium at Athens was used for the Panathenaic Games, and a faithful restoration in marble was carried out for the Olympic Games of 1906. The length of the course is 670 feet (= a "stadion," the ancient Greek measure of distance). Extending round the stadium in horse-shoe form are forty-four tiers of seats, with accommodation for as many as 50,000 spectators.

N. Zographos

E.N.A.

THE PROPYLÆA, GRANDEST OF GATEWAYS

The chief glory of non-religious Athenian architecture was the Propylæa, or entrance gateway to the Acropolis. Begun in 437 B.C., it consists of a square hall, with five passage-ways and nobly designed Doric colonnades on both the outer and the inner side. Originally it was designed to be flanked with projecting wings, but only one of these wings was ever completed.

THE TOWER OF THE WINDS

Erected during the Roman rule in Athens, the Tower of the Winds is an elegant marble structure, once fitted with a water-clock, sundials and a weathervane. Its eight sides face the points of the compass and are adorned with reliefs representing the various winds. The weathervane, on the roof, was in the form of a Triton.

Robert Byron

AMAZING MONASTERIES OF ATHOS

One of the strangest communities in the world is that grouped around Mount Athos, a beautiful mountain rising to 6,350 feet above the Aegean. Twenty Greek monasteries house three thousand monks and four thousand lay brothers, and are famous for their libraries and Byzantine art treasures. That of Simopetra, shown here, rising sheer from the top of a rocky eminence, is typical of their astounding architecture.

E.N.A.

E. O. Hoppé

FOUR - THOUSAND - YEAR - OLD THRONE AT KNOSSOS

The Royal Palace at Knossos, constructed about 2100 B.C., is the most important monument of "Minoan" civilization (called after the mythical king Minos). Within it is this remarkable throne of gypsum, the oldest throne in the world, with a leaf-shaped back and the seat hollowed out for comfort. Stone benches encircle the room, which is decorated with mural paintings.

COLOSSAL MASONRY AT MYCENÆ

Among the ruins of Mycenæ, the city of Agamemnon, is the famous Lion Gate, forming the entrance to the Acropolis and dating from about 1400 B.C. The huge lintel is 16½ feet long, 8 feet wide and 3 feet thick, and on it rests a slab of limestone (12 feet wide, 10 high and 2 thick) carved with a relief of two heraldic lions, one on either side of a cylindrical column.

F. Henle

AN EXQUISITE TEMPLE OF VICTORY

The Temple of the Wingless Victory—or, rather, that of Athena Victorious—here seen through the columns of the Propylæa, stands on a bastion of the Acropolis at Athens and, though a reconstruction, is perhaps the finest of the smaller Hellenic temples. It is built entirely of Pentelic marble and was probably set up to commemorate the Athenian and Grecian victories over the Persians in the fifth and fourth centuries B.C.

THE POLISH NATIONAL CATHEDRAL AT CRACOW

The Gothic Cathedral of St. Stanislaus at Cracow, consecrated in 1359, is Poland's Westminster Abbey. For here the kings of Poland were crowned; and here rest the remains of the patron saint of the Poles, St. Stanislaus, besides those of the kings of Poland and the country's greatest sons (e.g., John Sobieski, Kosciuszko, Poniatowski). Here, too, a portion of the ancient regalia is kept.

A CHAPEL CARVED FROM SALT

The salt-mines at Wieliczka, near Cracow, are the most productive in Europe, yielding about 60,000 tons annually and employing more than one thousand hands. There are over 65 miles of galleries on seven different levels, the lowest 980 feet deep. The wonderful underground chapel of St. Kenga, hewn out of the rock-salt, has its altars, candelabra, and all other similar fittings also carved in salt.

E.N.A.

Wide World

Mondiale Foto-press

THE IRON GATES

In its passage through the Transylvanian Alps on its way to the Black Sea, the Danube flows through a last defile, the celebrated Iron Gates. Two miles in length, its scenery is of a sombre magnificence.

TOKEN OF BULGARIAN GRATITUDE TO RUSSIA

The grand Cathedral of St. Alexander Nevski, the largest modern church in the Balkans, standing in the centre of Sofia, was erected (1896–1912) in memory of the Russians who fell in the war with Turkey 1877–1878, which gave independence to Bulgaria. Alexander Nevski was a thirteenth-century Russian hero and saint, victor on many occasions over Swedish forces and the Teutonic knights.

Lubinski

LAND OF A THOUSAND LAKES

A great part of the interior of Finland is covered by water and the country is famous for its innumerable and beautiful lakes. Here is a typical scene from an aerial viewpoint, the Punkaharju, an extraordinary wooded ridge 4½ miles long, winding tortuously between the two lakes of Saima and Puruvesi.

Lubinski

HELSINKI CENTRAL—WORLD-RENOWNED RAILWAY STATION

Helsinki, better known under its old name, Helsingfors, is famed among the capitals of Europe for the excellence and originality of its modern architecture. The Central Railway Station, completed in 1919, is a particularly successful design, with its clock tower 157 feet in height and its impressive entrance archway. In the background stands the imposing colonnaded front of the Finnish Parliament House.

E.N.A.

MOSCOW'S CORONATION CHURCH

The Cathedral of the Assumption, standing in the centre of the Kremlin at Moscow, was the Coronation church of the Tsars and the burial-place of the Patriarchs of Moscow, chief dignitaries of the national church. Built between 1475 and 1479, it has five gilded domes, the central one 138 feet in height.

E.N.A.

IVAN VELIKI AND THE TSAR BELL

The bell tower of Ivan Veliki in the Kremlin, built by Tsar Boris Godunov in 1600, houses a famous carillon of thirty-three bells the largest of which weighs 65 tons. In the foreground stands the largest bell in the world, weighing 200 tons. Cast in 1735, it was cracked by fire before it could be hung.

W.G.W.—F

THE WALLS AND SPIRES OF THE

" There is nothing above Moscow except the Kremlin, and nothing above the Kremlin except Heaven." The Kremlin, or Citadel, of Moscow is a veritable city within a city, a triangular precinct enclosing a mass of splendid buildings—palaces, government offices, courts of justice, cathedrals and churches, arsenal

E.N.A.

KREMLIN—A CITY WITHIN A CITY

and barracks—surrounded by a 65-foot brick wall, $1\frac{1}{4}$ miles long. This picture shows the view of the Kremlin from the bridge over the River Moskva. In the centre is the Imperial Palace. The Kremlin remained virtually undamaged throughout the attacks launched by the German Air Force on Moscow in 1941.

Planet

THE GREAT DNIEPER DAM AT ZAPOROZHE

The River Dnieper, in its passage across the Ukraine, forces its way through a granite offshoot of the Carpathians, falling 155 feet in 25 miles. The Soviet Government constructed a colossal dam here between 1922 and 1927. Rather than surrender this great plant to the Germans, the Red Army destroyed it in 1941. Here it is shown during its reconstruction, which was completed in 1947.

E.N.A.

PALACE OF INDUSTRY AT KHARKOV

Kharkov was chosen in 1920 to be the capital of the Ukraine S.S.R. Administrative buildings were lacking, so an imposing Palace of Industry was erected, to accommodate both the offices of the Government and those of the great industrial undertakings. It consists of a complex array of buildings, with fourteen storeys in some cases and a total of over 4,000 rooms. Though badly damaged by the Germans during the 1939–45 War, its restoration was almost completed within three years of the cessation of hostilities.

E.N.A.

HUMAN BEE-HIVE IN THE CAUCASUS

Amazing though it appears to Western eyes, this Northern Caucasian town, Kubachi, has a history of more than a thousand years. More remarkable still, it is a centre for the production of cutlery and jewellery. Its appearance presents an extraordinary contrast to the new industrial cities of Soviet Russia.

E.N.A.

SUMMER PALACE OF RUSSIA'S TSARS

The village of Tsarskoye Selo (" The Tsar's Village ") was presented by Peter the Great to his wife Catherine. It became a summer residence for the Russian Imperial family, and was the earliest Russian town to be supplied with the conveniences of modern civilization. The picture shows the elaborate Palace which was designed by Guarenghi for Catherine II and built between 1792 and 1796. The Palace was extensively looted during that period in the 1939–45 War when Tsarskoye Selo was in the fighting zone.

E.N.A.

TO EXPIATE A TSAR'S ASSASSINATION

The Church of the Resurrection at Leningrad was erected on the spot where Alexander II was mortally wounded by Nihilist bombs on the very day (March 13, 1881) on which he had signed a decree of reform. Built of granite, marble and coloured brick, with nine domes each differing from the others (the highest reaching a height of 266 feet), it is decorated with an amazing profusion of mosaic, gilding and enamel. Damaged during the fighting around Leningrad in 1941 and 1942, it was restored after the War.

ST. SOPHIA, ONCE CHRISTENDOM'S GREATEST CHURCH

The "Church of the Holy Wisdom," built A.D. 532–537, is most sumptuously decorated with marble and mosaics. Some 360 cwt. of gold is said to have been used, and 10,000 workmen engaged on its construction. After the capture of Constantinople by the Turks, A.D. 1453, it was converted into a mosque. Here is a view of the lavish interior under the great dome, 185 feet in height.

Ullstein

THE OLD WALLS OF CONSTANTINOPLE

The Town Walls of Constantinople, constructed by Theodosius II in the fifth century, stretch from the Sea of Marmora to the Golden Horn, over four miles. Consisting of a triple enceinte, in all 200 feet wide and 100 feet high, strengthened originally by 192 towers and a 60-foot moat, they form the most colossal system of medieval town defences ever carried out.

E.N.A.

THE GOLDEN HORN AND

The Mosque of Sultan Suleiman I (1550–1556), the finest built by the Turks in Constantinople, now Istanbul, was modelled on St. Sophia, which was to be put in the shade as regards size and costliness. Its clustered domes and minarets certainly make a more effective exterior. Behind it lies the Golden Horn,

E.N.A.

THE SULEIMAN MOSQUE

the city's magnificent natural harbour, formed by an arm of the Bosporus and spanned by the New Bridge. In length (512 yards) and amount of traffic (over 150,000 persons cross it daily in spite of a toll) it is one of the world's greatest bridges. Constructed in 1912 at a cost of £250,000, it is supported by iron pontoons.

Australian Trade Publicity

A NATURAL SHAWL

The south-west coast of Western Australia is literally honeycombed with huge caves, transformed into fairy palaces by Nature's silent work through the centuries. The principal cave, situated at Yallingup, 20 miles from Busselton, is of immense size. Brilliantly lighted by electricity, the interior displays a marvellous series of stalactites and stalagmites; its strange "shawls" are the finest in existence.

OCEANIA

The term Oceania applies to territories which are distributed over an enormous area of ocean, but in point of land surface they cover less than 3,500,000 square miles and Oceania is thus the smallest of the continents. Included in these territories are Australia, New Zealand and a myriad islands scattered over the Pacific, but for purposes of convenience in treatment the sub-continent of Antarctica has been considered with them in this book.

Antarctica, the region round the South Pole, is itself almost half as large again as the whole of Oceania, for it covers the enormous area of nearly 5,000,000 square miles.

AN ICE-CLAD TABLELAND

Lying wholly within the Antarctic Circle, it is undoubtedly the most inhospitable land on earth, consisting of an illimitable plateau some 3,000 to 4,000 feet in average height, covered for the most part by one vast sheet of ice, in places 1,500 feet thick. Here nothing grows except a few mosses and lichens; here nothing lives except on the fringes of the sea, where innumerable penguins and seals live on the ice-floes and small islets. Within the sea itself, however, life teems, for contrary to popular belief the polar are far more densely populated than the tropical seas.

Man has small place here and his achievements have been recorded only in feats of endurance and courage. Nature alone is the wonder-worker, and her fashioning of ice and snow is awe-inspiring and often breath-taking in its loveliness. In the amazing icebergs, floating like small islands on those arctic seas, in the precipices of the Ross Barrier, for example, rearing their ice-edges hundreds of feet in the air for mile after endless mile at the sea edge, in the mighty glaciers such as the Barne, no less than in her sport with titanic volcanoes, such as Mount Erebus, thrusting their smoke-laden cones thousands of feet above the snow and ice on their lower slopes, Nature has wrought wonders comparable with any on the globe.

By far and away the major part of Oceania proper is comprised in Australia, the largest island of the world, some 2,974,000 square miles in area. Its age-long separation from the rest of the earth's surface has produced remarkable results in the way of evolution, for its animal and plant life, and even its few aboriginal inhabitants, are quite unique. Here are found such ancient survivals as the marsupial or pouched animals, kangaroos and wombats, primitive egg-laying mammals like the duck-billed platypus, and distinctive plants and trees like the sweet-smelling "wattle" (mimosa), and valuable timber like the jarrah and karri trees.

Today, the population of Australia amounts to about 7,580,000—a small number for so vast an area. But because the best land is on the coastal fringe, the population has concentrated in the main cities and in areas relatively near the coast; nearly half the people live in the six state capitals.

Australia is the world's chief exporter of wool, and one of the world's four biggest suppliers of wheat, meat, butter, dried fruit, canned fruits and apples.

The problem of water supply is being tackled with real energy, and the harnessing of the great Murray and Murrumbidgee rivers has brought more people to many of the low-rainfall areas, and has helped the expansion of the dried and canned fruit industries. Further development of these industries depends on world markets. The planting of vines and canning of fruits is government-controlled, and these controls are unlikely to be relaxed until further world markets are found.

But although rural industries provide the major share of the national income, Australia is pinning her faith to increased manufactures in the effort to raise her population to 20,000,000. Abundant new materials and the undeveloped markets of the East are attracting considerable British and American capital to Australia, and many new enterprises are going forward.

AN ENGINEERING MARVEL

Chief of all the engineering wonders which man has created in Australia is the magnificent Sydney Harbour Bridge, spanning perhaps the finest natural harbour in the world. The Hawkesbury River Bridge is another triumph of engineering, and one must mention, too, the construction of the Trans-continental Railway, which, running from east to west, opened up the gold-mining areas round Coolgardie, Kalgoorlie and elsewhere, the Overland Telegraph from north to south and the mighty cities on the east and south-east coast, Melbourne, Sydney, Adelaide and the rest.

Photographic Publications

FAMOUS VIEW THROUGH THE CARLOTTA ARCH

The Jenolan Caves, situated in one of the valleys of the Blue Mountains, are the most extensive limestone caverns in Australia and are remarkable for their stalactite formations. The view from inside the huge Carlotta Arch (which forms the entrance to these caverns) is acclaimed as one of the finest in Australia.

The capital of Australia is, however, Canberra, situated within a special Federal territory lying in the state of New South Wales, a capital city of barely 15,000 inhabitants, consisting of little more than the impressive group of Parliament Buildings for the legislature and secretariat of the Australian Commonwealth.

VAST CATTLE RANCHES

It is Nature, however, who has provided man with his greatest opportunities, for she is the real author of those wonderful wheat fields and the sheep and cattle ranches which cover hundreds of thousands of square miles of Australian territory. Elsewhere she has worked more hardly; the central desert has already been mentioned, but as an awe-inspiring subject it is rivalled if not surpassed by the Great Barrier Reef, that astonishing natural breakwater, mainly of coral formation, stretching for over 1,200 miles along the eastern coast.

Australia has no great mountain ranges except the Great Dividing Range in the east, the highest summit of which is Mount Kosciusko (7,300 feet); but in the Blue Mountains, a part of the Range, is some of the world's most glorious scenery, and no other country in the world can boast such a wonderful system of natural limestone caverns, which include such remarkable caves as those at Yallingup in Western Australia and Jenolan in the Blue Mountains.

New Zealand, a thousand miles from Australia, consists of two major islands, North and South, both of almost incomparable natural beauty, and a host of outlying dependencies. Its total area of about 100,000 square miles is somewhat larger than Great Britain's and it is blessed with a climate acclaimed as the finest in the world, with a moderate rainfall and an equable temperature. Nature has smiled on this little territory in truth, and its industrious people—almost all of British stock except for the original Maoris (a brave and very intelligent race)—have laboured so well that in dairy farming New Zealand now rivals Denmark, and in cattle and, particularly, sheep-rearing is, for its size, one of the leading countries in the world.

North Island, which contains 65 per cent of the total population of about 1,800,000, possesses two wonderful natural harbours at Auckland and at Wellington, the capital of the country. It is world-famous, moreover, for the amazing hot spring district round Lake Taupo and Rotorua, an area of 5,000 square miles. Here volcanic phenomena can be seen in their most startling beauty, and although the famous Pink and White Terraces were lamentably destroyed in the eruption of 1886, yet there remain marvels in almost unlimited profusion. Boiling pools, geysers, mud volcanoes, lakes and waterfalls of exquisite beauty attract visitors from all over the world. Here are the volcanoes Mount Ruapehu (9,175 feet) and extinct Mount Egmont, the Fujiyama of New Zealand.

South Island presents an interesting contrast to the fertile pastures that cover most of North Island. On the coastal plains, it is true, are found rich corn and cattle lands; but the whole of the north-western portion of the island is occupied by the Southern Alps, range upon range of magnificent peaks capped in perpetual snow and ice. Aorangi, or Mount Cook (12,349 feet), commemorating the famous navigator, is the greatest and is also one of the world's most impressive mountains, but there are countless others. South Island has mighty glaciers such as the Tasman, lakes and mountain torrents in extravagant profusion of wild beauty and waterfalls such as the Sutherland and Bowen Falls, which would grace any mountain scenery in the world. The height of sublime grandeur is reached in the salt-water Sounds of the south-west coast. Milford Sound and Dusky Sound are the most celebrated.

ISLANDS OF ETERNAL SUMMER

The remainder of Oceania consists of those thousands of groups of islands which lie scattered across the 5,000 and more miles of ocean separating Australia from America. They are world-famed for the eternal summer of their climate, for the physical beauty and charm of their dark-skinned inhabitants and for the loveliness of their coral strands and their palm-trees. Many are highly volcanic, more are coralline, and some are both. The world's greatest active volcanic crater is Kilauea on Hawaii, and the world's finest coral reefs are on the island of Loh. Man's handiwork, modern or ancient, is but little in evidence unless it be in the extensive pineapple plantations on such islands as Hawaii; the exceptions are that mysterious arch of three great stones on Tonga Island and the idols on Easter Island.

Oceania cannot claim to rival in number the man-made and natural marvels of which other continents can boast, but it need yield to few in the wonder of those which it has to show.

Australian National Travel Association

PARLIAMENT HOUSE OF THE COMMONWEALTH OF AUSTRALIA

Canberra, in New South Wales, was chosen in 1909 as the seat of the Federal Government. An area of 1,200 square miles was vested in the Commonwealth, and work was begun in 1913 on the Federal City, including the Parliament buildings. This view shows the main drive in front of the imposing façade of the new building, which was formally opened by George VI, then Duke of York, in May, 1927.

Australian Official Photograph

ULTRA-MODERN BRIDGE, 2,000 FEET LONG

This steel bridge over the Hawkesbury River, in New South Wales, is 2,005 feet long and the steelwork weighs 2,180 tons. An outstanding product of Australia's heavy industries, the bridge was built at the works in sections, the largest of which weighed 24 tons, and transported by road to the river site.

Photographic Publications

STRANGE CORAL GROWTHS OF THE GREAT BARRIER REEF

The Great Barrier Reef, which runs parallel with the Queensland coast at a distance of 20 to 70 miles, is the largest coral reef in the world, being over 1,200 miles long. This natural breakwater covers an area of 100,000 square miles. All coral is built up, not as is popularly supposed by "coral insects," but from the hard skeletons (composed of carbonate of lime from the sea) of marine organisms, chiefly polyps.

Australian Trade Publicity

TESSELLATED STALACTITES

Amongst the other famous subterranean caverns between Yallingup and Augusta are the Margaret Caves, in the vicinity of the Margaret River. The chief of these is the celebrated Lake Cave, which for the sheer fairylike loveliness of its formations is considered to be without peer anywhere in the Commonwealth.

THE VAST EXPANSE OF SYDNEY

Sydney, capital of New South Wales and oldest of Australian cities, was founded by Governor Philip in 1788 on one of the world's finest natural harbours. Deep and sheltered, easily defensible yet easily accessible from the sea, it covers an enormous area and provides moreover a magnificent pleasure resort for the 1½ million residents in the Sydney area. Transport across the harbour was carried on entirely by

Australian National Travel Association

HARBOUR AND ITS FAMOUS BRIDGE

ferries until 1932, when Sydney Bridge, the world's second greatest single-arch bridge, was opened, after eight years' work. Its total length is 3,770 feet, while the main arch measures 1,650 feet. The bridge, which is built of silicon steel, carries a 57-foot roadway, two footways and four lines of railway. The clearance above high water is 170 feet. This picture shows its value to Sydney's communications.

Wide World

THE FRANZ JOSEF GLACIER—MIGHTY RIVER OF ICE AND SNOW

The Franz Josef Glacier, named in honour of the late Austrian emperor, is one of the most famous of the glaciers that beautify the Southern Alps of New Zealand. Descending from the western slopes of Mount Cook, it winds its way through the forests before finally melting away at a point only 400 feet above sea-level.

Ullstein

FAIRYLAND IN AN ICE CAVERN

The Tasman Glacier, the greatest among the Southern Alps, is 18 miles in length, with an average width of a mile and a quarter. This picture shows a view from inside an ice-cavern of fairylike beauty. The glacier is fitly named after the Dutch navigator who discovered New Zealand on December 13, 1642.

Fox

WATER-BUILT CONE OF A FAMOUS GEYSER

In the North Island of New Zealand there exists a hot spring district, celebrated for its geysers and mud volcanoes. Amongst its famous geysers is that known as Waikite, which throws a column of boiling water to a height of 35 feet. It is remarkable for its curiously shaped cone, built up of siliceous deposits.

Fox

A GEYSER THAT SPOUTED STEAM NEARLY A THIRD OF A MILE HIGH

Chief amongst the geyser-basins of the hot spring district is Waimangu, the largest pool of boiling water on earth, set in a scene of volcanic splendour. In the final eruption that destroyed it, the geyser cast up a column consisting of mud, stones, boiling water and steam to a height of some 1,500 feet.

E.N.A.

THE BOILING MUD CRATERS OF THE TIKITERE VALLEY

Amongst the other volcanic wonders of the Rotorua hot spring district are the lakes or craters of boiling mud found chiefly in the Tikitere Valley. This picture shows a view looking down into one of these craters. Note the characteristic whirlpool formations set up by the eruption of huge bubbles of steam.

E.N.A.

LIKE A BUBBLING CAULDRON OF CHAMPAGNE

One of the most famous of New Zealand's hot springs is the Great Geyser of Wairakei, which ejects a column of water—sometimes as high as 40 feet—at regular intervals of eight minutes. The pale-brown spongy masses of sinter deposit around its outflow have won it the name of the Champagne Cauldron.

THE MYSTERIOUS AND MONSTROUS

Rapanui, or Easter Island, 2,000 miles from Chile and 1,100 from Pitcairn Island, is the remotest outpost of the Polynesian race. The Dutch admiral, Roggeveen, was the first European to land there—on Easter Sunday, 1722. Though the native population is now reduced to about 150, a highly cultured race must at one time have occupied the island—to judge from the extraordinary number of sculptured

Ewing Galloway

SCULPTURES OF EASTER ISLAND

monuments still to be seen there, and from the remains of their unique picture-writing. It is still a subject of conjecture how such great masses of stone (up to 50 tons in weight) were transported from the quarries at the north-east end of the island. There are in all no fewer than 260 burial platforms on the island, and these are surrounded in some cases by as many as fifteen sculptures (presumably statues of ancestors).

Paul Popper

MOUNT EREBUS, AN ICE-CLAD VOLCANO

On Ross Island, one of an archipelago of volcanic islands in the Ross Sea, is Mount Erebus, the largest of a group of active volcanoes. Its height above sea-level is estimated at about 13,000 feet, and despite the fact that it is almost always in eruption it is snow-covered right up to the tip of its crater. Contrary to popular expectation, the Antarctic seas teem with life, as is evidenced by the penguins in this picture.

Paul Popper

A VAST ICE TABLE IN THE SEA

The icebergs of the Antarctic regions assume for the most part a characteristic tabular form, due to the fact that the ocean swell breaks them off in summer from the flat-topped floating sheets of ice of enormous area known as barriers, such as the Ross Barrier and others. The icebergs may reach a height of 200 feet.

Paul Popper

THE BARNE GLACIER'S STUPENDOUS ICE PRECIPICE

In Barne Inlet, Victoria Land, between the Ross Sea and the South Pole, is a glacier which probably contains more ice than any other in the world. Yet the Barne Glacier is receding, and at one time was three to four thousand feet above its present level. The height of its present ice face is estimated at 280 feet.

Paul Popper

TOWERING WALLS OF A MIGHTY ICE CAVERN

Antarctica, a vast land mass over half as big again as Europe, rises to an average level of over 4,000 feet, covered by an ice-sheet some 1,500 feet thick, and is far more inclement than the north polar regions. Here Nature works strange freaks, such as this colossal ice cavern formed in the sea-face of a slow-moving glacier.

THE AMERICAS

THE great American continent which occupies the western hemisphere is longer from north to south than any other land-mass on the globe. In the centre, however, it narrows to the strip of land known as the Isthmus of Panama, which divides it into twin continents, North and South America, of strikingly similar outline, broad in the North and tapering in the south, and roughly identical in their geological conformation. Each has a great mountain range running parallel to its western coast, with a consequent absence of westward-flowing rivers; and each possesses one of the world's greatest rivers—the Missouri–Mississippi and the Amazon respectively.

Farthest north lies Canada, a federation of provinces and a self-governing dominion of the British Commonwealth, slightly larger than the United States and slightly smaller than Europe.

More than a million square miles in the maritime provinces of Eastern Canada, in British Columbia and in the unsettled areas of the north are covered with forests of spruce, producing inexhaustible supplies of lumber, firewood, pit-props and pulp for newsprint.

The chief wealth of the country, however, lies in the three central provinces of Manitoba, Saskatchewan and Alberta. Here are found those amazing, almost limitless wheatfields which produce a great part of the wheat which comes on to the international market.

The Rocky Mountains, farther west, and the Selkirk and Coastal Ranges of British Columbia have a wealth of scenery to offer such as is not to be found in any other part of the world.

The great cities of Canada lie mostly in the east: Quebec, the French city of historic memories, proudly sited at the mouth of the St. Lawrence; Montreal and Toronto, great commercial centres; Ottawa, the capital, with its impressive Parliament Buildings. In the realm of civil engineering Canada can proudly point to some of the finest modern bridges in the world, at Quebec, Montreal, Vancouver, to such canals as the Welland Ship Canal, uniting Lakes Erie and Ontario, to the Connaught and other railway tunnels, and, above all, to its two great railway systems, the Canadian Pacific and Canadian National.

Canada shares with its neighbour, the United States, two of America's greatest natural wonders—the Great Lakes, which form the largest existing area of fresh water in the world, and the far-famed Niagara Falls.

The extreme north-western part of the continent is the territory of Alaska, once a Russian possession, but bought, with all its potentialities of fish, fur, gold, minerals and pulpwood, by the United States in 1867 for the derisory sum of under £1,500,000.

LAND OF THE FREE

Young country though it is, the United States was the first of modern republics, declaring its independence in 1776. The limits of its present territory, three million square miles, were not reached until 1850, after the discovery of gold in California had led to the development of the Pacific coast. The welcome then extended to all comers is symbolized by the gigantic statue of Liberty at the entrance of New York Harbour. The population, only four millions in 1800, is today more than 140 millions.

The scenic marvels of the United States equal those of Canada. By common consent the most wonderful spectacle on earth is the Grand Canyon of the Colorado River in Arizona, with its stupefying dimensions; as long as from London to Newcastle, wider than Central London, and 6,000 feet deep, with every colour of the rainbow in its rock strata. The largest of the National Parks is the Yellowstone, in Montana, a wonderland of geysers, coloured terraces, mud springs, waterfalls and a canyon of intensely vivid colouring. The Yosemite Valley, guarded by its great mountains, El Capitan and the Three Brothers, possesses the highest of the world's greater waterfalls, besides the Bridal Veil, of transcendent beauty, and other famous falls. Add to these the Garden of the Gods, Death Valley, the Painted Desert, Crater Lake, the Natural Bridges of Utah, the Big Trees of California, the Indian villages and cliff-dwellings of Arizona; still you have barely scratched the surface of the natural wonderland in the Far West. Such is the plethora of marvels that only a bare mention can be made here of the world's greatest cavern, the Mammoth Cave of Kentucky.

In the realm of human achievement, particularly as regards engineering, the United States holds many of the world records. New

Fairchild Aerial Surveys

THE TALLEST BUILDING IN THE WORLD

Towering above all its fellow skyscrapers, the Empire State Building in New York is the highest work of human hands in the world. Completed in 1931, it has 102 storeys, surmounted by a mooring mast for airships, the top of which is 1,248 feet above the level of the street. Express lifts take sightseers to the top platform, which commands a magnificent view over the whole city and environs for miles around.

York rivals London as the greatest city and greatest seaport on earth. Forced by exigencies of space to build upwards instead of outwards, the New Yorkers have made an architectural merit of necessity and erected a group of steel-framed skyscrapers which form what is certainly one of the most startling sights in the world —New York's skyline as seen from the harbour by the visitor arriving by ocean liner from Europe. Dominating everything is the Empire State Building, the highest structure so far erected by human hands. In bridge and tunnel building, too, New York can point to some of the most daring constructions ever attempted.

The capital of the United States is Washington, in the Federal District of Columbia, which was purchased for the express purpose in 1790. It is laid out in the grand manner, with the Capitol and the Library of Congress as the chief of its white stone and marble buildings in the classical style.

A RIVAL TO NEW YORK

Chicago, with its stockyards and meat-packing factories, rivals New York in wealth and in the number of its skyscrapers, and indeed is one of the busiest commercial centres in the universe. The Civic Opera House and the Lake Shore Drive, two of Chicago's chief ornaments, are both marvels of engineering. San Francisco has to its credit two of the world's boldest experiments in bridge-building, while other striking engineering achievements are the superb undertakings of the Boulder and Roosevelt Dams.

Mexico is a Federal Republic of twenty-eight states, and with its tropical lowlands, temperate plateaux and cold highlands has an extraordinarily varied climate, with a bewildering variety of vegetation. The capital, Mexico City, whose name commemorates that of the Aztec god of war, lies in the fertile Vale of Mexico, in full view of the gigantic snow-clad cone of Popocatepetl. This is one of the great Andean chain of smoking or silent volcanoes which extend almost unbroken from the United States border to the southern extremity of Chile. The earliest known civilization in Mexico is that of the Mayas; the architectural remains they have left at Copán, Chichen Itza and elsewhere show a wonderful proficiency in building and stone-carving in low relief.

In 1201 the Toltecs, who were perhaps a Maya tribe, captured Chichen Itza and there erected some of their step pyramids of stone, which were crowned with temples and arranged around open courts filled with enormous single stone columns and altars.

Under Spanish rule the church, here as elsewhere in Spanish America, wielded enormous power, and at one time is said to have owned half the wealth of the country. It was this wealth that made possible the erection of those magnificent cathedrals and churches, such as those at Mexico City, Puebla and Taxco, whose architectural merits rank them amongst the chief wonders of the country.

Central America, divided between the independent republics of Guatemala, Honduras, Salvador, Nicaragua, Costa Rica and Panama, with the British colony of Honduras on the Mosquito Coast, is a region of marvellous fertility and scenic beauty, with numerous volcanoes and lakes, but largely covered with undeveloped jungle. As yet it is but little developed, and man has few achievements here which can rank with the splendours of nature.

There is, however, one exception. At the point where the American continent narrows to a width of only forty miles, at Panama, it is severed by the world's most important canal, the successful completion of which by United States engineers was a triumph over every conceivable obstacle.

PEOPLE OF THE SUN

The northernmost country of South America, Colombia, has ports on two oceans, vast mineral wealth and what may prove to be the world's largest potential oilfield. Ecuador, the Republic of the Equator, an undeveloped state, with a population which is more than half purely Indian, is dominated by the peaks of Chimborazo and Cotopaxi, the highest of the numerous volcanoes that are here strung along the Andean chain.

When the Spanish explorers saw the Indian pile-dwellings on the shores of Lake Maracaibo they were impelled to call the country Venezuela, "little Venice." This pastoral, backward country has produced in the railway and road which run from La Guaira, the chief seaport, to Caracas, the capital, one of the greatest engineering achievements of modern times. Adjoining Venezuela are the three small colonies of British, Dutch and French Guiana, the only European holdings in South America. In British Guiana, however, is found

Canadian Pacific Railway

THE ROMANCE OF THE CANADIAN PACIFIC

In face of tremendous physical and financial difficulties, the C.P.R. from Montreal to the Pacific was completed in five years, the last spike being driven on November 7, 1885. Trains now run from Montreal to Vancouver, 2,882 miles, in 88 hours. The last six hundred miles, from Banff onwards, through the Rocky Mountains, traverse such scenery as this, unsurpassed for grandeur by any other railway on earth.

one of nature's greatest works, the Kaieteur Falls, which are among the highest of all the world's waterfalls of comparable size and volume.

About two thousand years ago the uplands of Peru and Bolivia were peopled by a race of Stone Age culture who were perhaps the finest stone-masons whom the world has ever seen. Their buildings, excellent examples of which are still extant at Tiahuanaco, on the shores of the great Lake Titicaca (that "Lake in the clouds"), and at Cuzco, were composed of great polygonal blocks, keyed in to each other and so perfectly fitting without the use of mortar that it is sometimes impossible to insert a penknife blade between them. In the thirteenth century Cuzco became the capital of the Incas, the famous " People of the Sun," whose empire, extending from Ecuador to Chile, was a kind of state socialism under the control of a supreme ruler regarded as a god on earth. Of the numerous remains of their colossal buildings the masterpiece is the Temple of the Sun at Cuzco, which now forms the base of the Spanish cathedral.

Bolivia, formerly Upper Peru, became a separate state in 1825, deriving its name from Bolivar, the great liberator. It lacks a coastline, but has the distinction of containing the highest inhabited land in the world and of having within its borders two of America's highest mountains, Illampu and Illimani.

BRAZIL'S LOVELY CAPITAL

More than half of South America belongs to Brazil, a federation of twenty-two states with an area greater than that of the U.S.A. Most of this great and fertile country, with its boundless resources of timber and minerals, is situated at a high altitude and suited for European occupation; the Amazon district, the largest river basin in the world, is entirely covered with a " green hell " of low-lying swampy forest, where hundreds of different species of trees, hung with parasitic plants of infinite diversity, create a stifling semi-darkness peopled chiefly by snakes, gaily plumed birds and myriads of stinging insects. One of the marvels of this great river is that sea-going steamers can ascend it as far as Iquitos in Peru, 2,300 miles from its mouth.

There can hardly be a fairer capital city than Rio de Janeiro, with its beautiful bay, its girdle of strikingly shaped mountains and its handsome squares and avenues and public buildings. One of its most remarkable peaks, the Sugarloaf, may be ascended by means of an aerial rope-railway, and another, the Corcovado, is crowned with a colossal figure of the Saviour. In the far south of Brazil—shared, in fact, with Argentina—are the vast Falls of the Iguazu.

Paraguay and Uruguay are two comparatively small cattle-ranching states. Uruguay has developed a considerable industry in meat-packing and the manufacture of beef extract. The centre of the trade is in its capital, Montevideo, a vast modern seaport dominated by the enormous tower of the tallest building in South America, the Palacio Salvo. For a century and a half Paraguay was under the complete spiritual and temporal domination of the Jesuits, many of whose churches are in a wonderful state of preservation.

A LAND OF CATTLE RANCHES

The southernmost and second largest country of South America is Argentina, whose great wealth lies in the vast, rolling pampas, flat treeless plains of great fertility both for cattle grazing and agriculture, which extend like the ocean for hundreds of miles in all directions. Buenos Aires, its splendid modern capital, is the third city of America.

A railway that opens up the magnificent scenery of the Andes—including such wonders as Aconcagua, long deemed the highest mountain in America, and Nature's strange handiwork, the Bridge of the Inca—unites Argentina with Chile. On the frontier stands the famous statue of Christ, erected to commemorate the friendly settlement of a dispute between the two countries over Patagonia.

Chile is latitudinally the longest country in America, and here the great barrier ranges of the Andes, with their snowy domes and glaciers, are of unexcelled dignity. Northern Chile is one of the driest countries in the world, being virtually rainless, but Nature's bounty has provided there a source of income on which the whole country's economy depends—beds of sodium nitrate sufficient to supply the world with fertilizers for decades to come.

The New World, as may be seen from this survey, is a wonderland of marvels. Nature, it is true, partly because of the vast scale on which she has worked, has taken pride of place; but man follows her closely, and in his feats of building and engineering he can claim to have created wonders in America which probably no other continent can rival. It is certain that none can surpass them.

Canada House

QUEBEC, OLDEST OF CANADA'S CITIES

Quebec has a high place among Canadian cities as much for its magnificent position at the mouth of the St. Lawrence as for its romantic history. The tall building is the Chateau Frontenac (a famous hotel), with the ancient Citadel crowning the plateau on the left. Behind the Citadel lie the Heights of Abraham, which are memorable as the scene of Wolfe's epoch-making victory over the French in 1759.

Canada House

A BRIDGE BUILT AT THE THIRD ATTEMPT

Quebec Bridge, crossing the St. Lawrence River at Cap Rouge, 9 miles above the city, was completed in 1917 after ten years' work and two collapses during its construction. It is 3,238 feet long and 88 feet wide, with the largest single cantilever span in the world (1,800 feet). The total cost was £1,800,000.

Photos : Fox

A BRIDGE
TWO MILES LONG

Begun in 1926 and finished in 1930, the Montreal Harbour Bridge, a double cantilever road bridge over the St. Lawrence River, was erected at a cost of twelve million dollars. Its total length, including approaches, exceeds two miles, and there is a head clearance of 163 feet. The bridge is wide enough to take four lanes of heavy traffic, besides two tram tracks and two footways for pedestrians.

MONTREAL'S
GREAT CHURCH

The Roman Catholic Church of Notre Dame was built in 1824 to replace an earlier church of 1672 and is one of the largest in America, accommodating a congregation of 12,000. The towers are 227 feet in height, and in the right-hand one hangs one of the heaviest bells in America, weighing over 12 tons. This view shows the west front of the cathedral. The statue in front commemorates Maisonneuve, who founded the city in 1642.

THE COMMERCIAL METROPOLIS OF

Founded by the French in 1642, and situated on an island in the St. Lawrence River, Montreal is the largest city in Canada and its commercial metropolis, though strangely it is not even the capital of a province. This view, taken from the beautiful Mount Royal Park, shows the business section of the city, whose skyline

Mondiale

CANADA AND ITS GREAT BRIDGE

is rapidly approximating to that of an American skyscraper town. The Victoria Bridge, seen in the background, crosses the St. Lawrence in twenty-five spans and is $1\frac{3}{4}$ miles in length; constructed in 1898–1899 at a cost of £4,000,000, it carries two railway tracks, an electric railway, two roadways and two footways.

Canadian Official News Bureau

SUMPTUOUS HOME OF CANADA'S PARLIAMENT

First built between 1859 and 1865 in a neo-Gothic style, the Parliament Buildings at Ottawa were utterly destroyed by fire in 1916. They were rebuilt immediately with an extra storey at a cost of $10,000,000. The actual Parliament house is in the centre—the wings are used as Government offices. The central tower is 285 feet high. In the background rises the spire of the celebrated Library building.

Fox

TORONTO'S TEN MILES OF WATERFRONT

The " Queen City," as Toronto is called, is the capital of Ontario Province and the second largest city in Canada. It extends for more than 10 miles along the shores of Lake Ontario, and this view shows the impressive skyline of its many tall buildings as seen across the Lake from the Island Park. Together with its extensive suburbs, it has a population which already approaches the million mark.

Canadian Pacific Railway

FIVE-MILE TUNNEL THROUGH A MOUNTAIN WALL

After negotiating the Rockies, the Canadian Pacific Railway encounters another barrier almost as formidable in the Selkirk Range of British Columbia, and to overcome this the Connaught Tunnel, 5 miles long and 3,787 feet above sea-level, was cut through a sheer rock face. The tunnel, which is double-tracked throughout, is drilled through the finest part of the range, situated in the Glacier National Park.

THE GREAT SWEEP OF NIAGARA,

Niagara is an Indian name meaning "Thunder of Waters," and the falls, shared between Canada and the United States, fully justify the description. The Niagara River, which forms the outlet to four of the Great Lakes, carries an enormous volume of water, 12 million cubic feet per minute, or about a

New York Times Photos

THE WORLD'S MOST FAMOUS FALLS

cubic mile weekly. The falls are divided by Goat Island into the Canadian or Horseshoe Fall, which is 2,550 feet wide and 158 feet high, and the American Fall, 1,000 feet wide and 167 feet high. Nine-tenths of the water goes over the former. The falls are used for power production by a large number of enterprises.

Fox

THE MANITOBA PARLIAMENT BUILDINGS AT WINNIPEG

The Parliament Buildings of Manitoba were built in the twentieth century. The buildings, which have been described as " a dream in stone," are approached by a magnificent avenue, the Victory Mall. On the right is a monument to Jacques Cartier, who established the first French settlement in Canada.

Canadian Official News Bureau

CONCRETE LOCKS TO BY-PASS NIAGARA

The Welland Ship Canal, 25 miles in length, was begun in 1913 and opened in 1931. It connects Lake Erie with Lake Ontario, by-passing the Niagara Falls and thus providing an outlet for sea-going steamers from the upper lakes via the St. Lawrence River to the Atlantic Ocean. To overcome a fall of 325 feet, seven locks (one of which is seen here) have been constructed, each 860 feet long by 80 feet wide.

Dorien Leigh

THE GREATEST FEAT OF BRIDGE ENGINEERING IN THE WORLD

The greatest combination bridge ever built unites San Francisco with Oakland. Its centre rests on Goat Island, through which the highway tunnels. The western crossing consists of suspension spans of 2,300 feet, with towers 440 feet in height. Opened on November 12, 1936, Oakland Bay Bridge, which is a two-decker structure throughout, has a total length of over 8 miles, and cost over £15,000,000.

Dorien Leigh

GREAT MOTOR HIGHWAY BENEATH A RIVER

Running from Canal Street, Manhattan, to Journal Square, Jersey City, the Holland Tunnel, designed by Clifford M. Holland, was begun in 1920 and opened in 1927. It has twin tunnels, each over 9,000 feet long and 29½ feet in diameter, each accommodating a double line of traffic. Over 60,000 vehicles can pass through daily. The total cost was $48,000,000. This view shows the dividing line between the states.

G.P.A.

MOST FAMOUS OF NEW YORK'S BRIDGES

Brooklyn Bridge connects New York with Brooklyn across the East River. Although it is now surpassed in size by other bridges, it has a span of 1,595 feet and a total length of 5,990 feet. Constructed in 1870–1883 at a cost of $15,000,000, it carries two railway tracks, two roadways and a wide raised footway.

E.N.A.

SPAN OF STEEL OVER 1,600 FEET LONG

The Kill van Kull is a tidal channel separating Staten Island from Jersey City. In 1931 a massive, arched bridge was opened between Bayonne, N.J., and Port Richmond, at an outlay of $16,000,000. Its arch span, 1,652 feet 1 inch, is the largest in the world, and 16,000 tons of steel were used in its construction.

AN OCEAN GIANT LEAVES THE MIGHTY DOCKS

New York is pre-eminent among the great seaports of the world; its landlocked harbour is admirably fitted by Nature for the reception of vessels of any size. The docks, situated close to the heart of the city, extend for miles on both sides of the south end of Manhattan Island, along the banks of the Hudson,

Paul Popper

OF THE WORLD'S GREATEST SKYSCRAPER CITY

or North River, and the East River. Both rivers are tidal, and the ocean liners berth at huge floating piers. In this picture the mighty liner *Queen Mary* is shown leaving the special pier which was constructed in New York Docks for her reception in 1936. In the background is seen crowded New York.

Fairchild Aerial Surveys

HISTORIC OBELISK ON WASHINGTON HILL

George Washington, chief creator of the United States, is worthily commemorated at the Federal city which bears his name by a unique monument of dignified simplicity — the Washington Obelisk. Built of white marble, it was begun in 1848 but not finished until 1884. It was built at a cost of $1,300,000 and measures 555 feet in height. A staircase of nine hundred steps and a lift provide an ascent to the top.

ABRAHAM LINCOLN'S MEMORIAL

Another great President of the United States, Abraham Lincoln, is commemorated at Washington—the scene of his assassination—this time by a Doric temple of white marble built in Potomac Park and inaugurated on May 30, 1922. It is 188 feet long and 118 feet wide, and its thirty-six columns represent the thirty-six states existing in Lincoln's time. Housed within the memorial is Daniel Chester French's statue of the President, the greatest upholder of the Union.

Underwood and Underwood

Fairchild Aerial Surveys

THE STATUE OF LIBERTY, GREETING NEW ARRIVALS TO AMERICA

Bedloe's Island, in New York Harbour, is dominated by the Statue of Liberty. Presented by the French Republic in commemoration of the centenary of the Declaration of Independence, it was designed by Bartholdi and erected in 1886. The dimensions are truly prodigious, for the height of the granite pedestal is 155 feet and of the copper and iron statue, 151 feet. The head can accommodate up to forty persons.

C. O. Buckingham

AMERICA'S HOUSES OF PARLIAMENT

The city of Washington is the capital of the United States, and its Capitol, or parliament building, is one of the world's most beautiful structures. Built of white marble and white-painted sandstone, it is surmounted by an iron dome, 268 feet high, crowned with a statue of Liberty. The building, which houses both the House of Representatives and the Senate of the United States, cost over $16,000,000.

THE MOST EXTENSIVE CAVES IN THE WORLD

The Mammoth Cave of Kentucky, really a whole series of caverns on five different levels, is the largest in the world, extending for 10 miles, with 150 miles of connecting passages. Within these vast caverns are stalagmites and stalactites, often of prodigious size. The stalactites shown in this picture are typical. It is estimated that in the carboniferous limestone area of Kentucky there are 100,000 miles of caves, still partly unexplored.

E.N.A.

MUSCLE SHOALS, FIRST INSTALMENT OF A TITANIC SCHEME

Muscle Shoals is a section of the Tennessee River, above Florence, Alabama, where the river drops 132 feet in 37 miles. Begun in 1918 and completed in 1925, the Wilson Dam is 4,300 feet in length, 107 feet high and 101 feet thick. The complete hydroelectric scheme of the Tennessee Valley Authority has been designed to add no less than 3,000,000 h.p. to the industrial resources of seven states.

Ewing Galloway

Lubinski

BUILDING WITH 100 ACRES OF FLOOR SPACE

Chicago is famed for its vast palaces of industry. The greatest of them, possibly the largest building in the world, is the Merchandise Mart or furniture repository, which, with a total floor space of 100 acres, is 744 feet in height and cost some $14,000,000 to build. Its central tower has twenty-five storeys.

E.N.A.

HEADQUARTERS OF A GREAT AUTOMOBILE ORGANIZATION

Detroit, founded by the French as far back as 1701, enjoys world-wide fame as the centre of the American automobile industry, founded by Robert E. Olds in 1899. Here is the home of one great motor company after another, including Ford Motors and the General Motors Corporation. The vast office building of the latter, an impressive view of which is shown here, is numbered amongst the largest buildings in the world.

E.N.A.

A SKYSCRAPER OPERA HOUSE

Chicago's twenty-million-dollar opera house in Wacker Drive was one of the enterprises of Samuel Insull, whose idea it was to combine a huge office-building with it, so that the rental of the offices should pay off the deficits incidental to opera. Finished in 1929, this sky-filling structure has forty-two storeys.

Ewing Galloway

PIKE'S PEAK, AMERICA'S MOST POPULAR MOUNTAIN

Perhaps the best-known mountain in the Rocky Mountains of America is Pike's Peak, discovered by Lieutenant Zebulon Pike in 1806. Although it is one of the highest summits in the United States, being 14,108 feet in height, it is ascended by a motor road (the highest in the world) and a cog-wheel railway.

Ewing Galloway

SANDSTONE SPIRES IN "THE GARDEN OF THE GODS"

Near the fashionable health-resort of Colorado Springs lies the celebrated Garden of the Gods, a tract of about 500 acres notable for its utterly fantastic group of bright red or white sandstone cliffs and rocks. The pinnacles known as the Cathedral Spires, seen in this picture, are over 300 feet in height. This area, part of a municipal park owned by the city of Colorado Springs, includes many similar formations.

Fairchild Aerial Surveys

THE WORLD'S BUSIEST CANAL

Lake Huron is connected with Lake Superior by the Strait called St. Mary's River, the rapids on which, opposite Sault-Ste-Marie, are avoided by means of the Soo Ship Canal. Begun in 1853 and constantly improved, this canal is 2,330 yards long, 108 feet wide and 16 feet deep. Its newest lock is 1,350 feet long and 80 feet wide. This view shows typical lake steamers congregated at the entrance to the canal.

Ewing Galloway

UNDERGROUND TEMPLES OF THE AZTECS

Important relics of the famous civilization of ancient Mexico are to be seen in the U.S.A., particularly in the state of New Mexico. This picture shows the excavated remains of an Aztec village, with large round holes known as kivas, where the Aztec Indians carried out their weird rites in underground temples.

E.N.A.

MODERNISTIC ARCHITECTURE IN PRIMITIVE DWELLINGS

The Pueblo Indians, both of the Zuni or Hopi tribes, have many communities in the " Sunshine State " of New Mexico. Their dwellings and their ways of life are of great interest to anthropologists and archæologists alike, and amongst the most interesting of their villages is this community house, at Pueblo de Taos, constructed of adobe (sun-dried brick). The beehive-shaped objects are bread ovens.

E.N.A.

TITANIC MOUNTAIN SCULPTURES COMMEMORATING FOUR PRESIDENTS

On the granite face of Mount Rushmore, in the Black Hills of South Dakota, is carved a gigantic figure of George Washington, executed by the celebrated American sculptor, Gutzon Borglum, a disciple of Rodin and a specialist in such work. Close by are similarly sculptured figures of Presidents Jefferson, Lincoln and Roosevelt. The whole memorial was dedicated by President Coolidge on August 10, 1927.

Dorien Leigh

Mondiale

UNIQUE TERRACES OF THE MAMMOTH HOT SPRINGS

Many of the wonders of Yellowstone Park are creations of volcanic activity, evidence of which survives in the presence of numerous hot springs and geysers. The most striking of these phenomena is a series of picturesque terraces formed by the deposits of calcium carbonate carried in solution by the seventy Mammoth Hot Springs. Every colour conceivable is to be found in these twelve terraces, which are 300 feet high and cover an area of 200 acres.

A GEYSER THAT SPOUTS 250 FEET IN THE AIR

Among the innumerable geysers of the Yellowstone Park, probably the greatest (in the park, as in the whole world) is the Giant Geyser, which works intermittently, at irregular intervals. It throws a huge mass of boiling water and steam to a height of 250 feet, the performance usually lasting for about an hour and a half.

Photochrom

THE GRAND CANYON OF THE YELLOWSTONE

Acclaimed as possibly the most impressive of all the natural wonders of the world is the Grand Canyon of the Yellowstone River, seen in this view taken from Inspiration Point, a famous belvedere. No photograph, of course, can convey any idea of its gorgeous colouring of red, orange, yellow and purple. The gigantic canyon varies in depth from 600 to 1,200 feet and in width from 900 to 4,500 feet. The Yellowstone River, flowing northward, plunges over two deep falls into the canyon which it has cut.

E.N.A.

THE MYSTERIOUS CLIFF PALACE OF THE MANCOS CANYON

In the remote wilds of Colorado is the Mesa Verde National Park, which has been established in order to secure the preservation of its cliff-dwellings, about which extremely little is known. The most imposing of these is the so-called Cliff Palace in the Mancos Canyon, which is in an excellent state of preservation.

G.P.A.

E.N.A.

NATURE SPANS A CHASM 205 FEET WIDE

The three Natural Bridges of Utah, situated in the San Juan River district, which is now a National Park, are world-famous. They are remarkable formations cut in the light sandstone rock of the district. The Edwin Bridge, which is shown above, with a span of 205 feet, and 111 feet in height, is actually the smallest but the most graceful of the three.

FANTASTIC FORMATION OF THE DEVIL'S SLIDE

The Echo and Weber Canyons, celebrated for their startling rock and mountain scenery, are situated in the " Enclosed Basin " of Utah, a great area of internal drainage and salt lakes. In the Weber Canyon is the extraordinary formation known as the Devil's Slide, consisting of two colossal outcrops of rock, descending in parallel lines to the river bank.

Fairchild Aerial Surveys

Paul Popper

MAN-MADE LAKE IN ARIZONA'S DESERTS

The famous Roosevelt Dam on the Salt River, near Globe, Arizona, providing irrigation for an exceptionally arid district, has turned a desert into one of the most fertile farming regions in the world. In the above aerial view it is to be seen as a small white patch situated at the point where the river leaves the reservoir. The lake formed by the dam has a capacity of 1,637,000 acre-feet.

WORLD-FAMOUS DAM ON THE COLORADO RIVER

Standing on the Colorado River at Boulder Canyon, Boulder Dam represents one of the greatest triumphs of modern engineering. Besides supplying millions with electric power and irrigating water (it has created the largest artificial lake in the world), it is used for flood control and regulating the flow of the lower Colorado River. Its base is 650 feet thick, tapering to 45 feet at the top, and it is 727 feet from foundation to crest.

E.N.A.

WORLD'S MOST SPECTACULAR CHASM

One of Nature's most awe-inspiring creations is certainly the Grand Canyon through which the River Colorado flows within the state of Arizona. Its length is 278 miles, its average width 10 miles and the height of its stupendous walls varies from 3,000 to no less than 6,000 feet. The latter, sculptured by erosion into the most fantastic shapes, are remarkable for the brilliance and variety of their colouring.

E.N.A.

600-FEET-DEEP MYSTERY CRATER

Near Sunshine, Arizona, is Crater Mound, an extraordinary crater-like hollow, measuring 4,000 feet in diameter and 600 feet in depth. Its rim rises 100 to 150 feet above the plain. Some authorities believe that it was caused by the fall of a meteorite, but others suggest it is due to an explosion of volcanic steam.

H. C. Tibbets

THE FAMOUS MORMON TEMPLE OF SALT LAKE CITY

Salt Lake City, now a state capital with 150,000 inhabitants, was founded in 1857 by the Mormons or Latter Day Saints, under Brigham Young. Their Temple is a magnificent granite building, completed in 1893 at a cost of over four million dollars. The tallest of its six spires attains a height of 220 feet. Behind it is the extraordinary oval-shaped Tabernacle, which can accommodate 12,000 worshippers.

Underwood and Underwood

A SHEER CLIFF FACE 3,000 FEET HIGH

Glacier Point in the Yosemite Valley, an illustration of which forms the frontispiece to this book, is the finest and most frequented view-point in America's grandest national park. This picture shows a less usual view—its aspect looking upwards from the floor of the valley over which the great rock hangs precariously. Small waterfalls dash down the face of the precipitous cliff, which is over 3,000 feet in height.

Ewing Galloway

E.N.A.

MOST FAMOUS OF THE CALIFORNIAN BIG TREES

Near Wawona, in California, is the Mariposa Grove, consisting of about six hundred specimens of the " Big Tree of California," *Sequoia gigantea*, the world's tallest tree, which sometimes attains a height of over 350 feet and a girth of 100 feet. A road-tunnel, 10 feet high and 10 feet wide, has been cut through the base of the Wawona Tree, which has so far attained 227 feet in height and 28 feet in diameter.

HIGHEST OF THE WORLD'S GREAT WATERFALLS

Prominent among the multifarious attractions of the Yosemite Valley are the Yosemite Falls, which are the highest in the world among waterfalls of comparable volume. Their three leaps have an aggregate height of 2,500 feet, of which the upper fall, with 1,436 feet, is by far the largest. The width at the top is 35 feet. The Yosemite National Park, half a million acres in area, comprises the whole watershed of the Yosemite Valley.

Mondiale

MASSED PINNACLES OF A FAMOUS CANYON

Bryce Canyon, in the south central part of Utah State, is an outstanding example of a " box " canyon, containing some remarkable examples of erosion; particularly striking are the stone pinnacles eroded by wind and sand into fantastic shapes. The surrounding area has been set apart as a National Park.

W.G.W.—H

Underwood and Underwood

THE WORLD'S LONGEST SUSPENSION BRIDGE—

The Golden Gate, entrance to San Francisco Bay, was bridged in 1937 after five years' labour and an expenditure of $32,000,000. The main span of the bridge measures 4,200 feet—a world's record—while each of the side spans is 1,125 feet and the total length 9,217 feet. The width is 90 feet, and the clearance above high water 220 feet. The principal suspension cables are 36½ inches in diameter!

E.N.A.

—AND THE WORLD'S BIGGEST CRATER LAKE

High up in the Cascade Mountains of Oregon lies Crater Lake, formed by the subsidence of an extinct volcano. It is five miles across and 2,000 feet deep, and the surrounding walls of rock are 2,000 feet high in places. Wizard Island, seen in this picture, is a curious instance of a cone within a crater.

E.N.A.

MEXICO'S NATURE-BUILT NATIONAL THEATRE

At San Juan Teotihuacan, thirty miles north-east of Mexico City and in the very shadow of the ancient Pyramid of the Sun, is a vast natural amphitheatre in the hillside. The site has been skilfully adapted as a National Open-Air Theatre and stone seats to accommodate several thousand have been built in.

E.N.A.

THE GREAT TERRACED PYRAMID OF THE SUN

The two great terraced pyramids or " teocallis " at San Juan Teotihuacan, dedicated to the Sun and the Moon respectively, are believed to be relics of the Toltec, or even a pre-Toltec, race. The Pyramid of the Sun, seen here, is 216 feet in height, and constructed of adobe bricks; its base measures 721 by 761 feet.

E.N.A.

THE MARVELLOUS STALACTITES OF CACAHUAMILPA

Discovered in 1835, the Cacahuamilpa Cave, in the Mexican state of Guerrero, is rivalled in size only by the Mammoth Cave of Kentucky, which it resembles in formation. It has 12,000,000 cubic yards of galleries, eleven lakes, seven rivers and eight waterfalls. No other cavern can show finer specimens of stalactites, which are formed by lime-containing water dripping from the roof, or of stalagmites, which grow upwards from the floor to meet the stalactites.

AN EIGHTEENTH-CENTURY SPANISH AQUEDUCT AT QUERETARO

The long aqueduct which conveys a copious water supply from the mountains to the Mexican city of Queretaro is a splendid engineering achievement, carried out between 1726 and 1738, in the period of Spanish rule. Some of its many arches are 100 feet high.

Ewing Galloway

E.N.A.

THE GREAT TEMPLE OF CHICHEN-ITZA

The so-called Castillo, or Castle, of Chichen-Itza, seen in this picture, was really the principal temple of the city, dedicated to the Plumed Serpent, the Mayan expression of which is Quetzalcoatl. It covers an acre of ground and rises 100 feet above the plain. Chichen-Itza was not finally abandoned till 1448.

Ewing Galloway

THE FAMOUS ARCHITECTURE OF TAXCO'S CHURCH

The great church of San Sebastian y Santa Prisca at Taxco in the Mexican state of Guerrero is the finest example of the distinctive architecture famous throughout Mexico, known as Chirrigueresque after the architect Chirriguera. Built by a silver-mining magnate at the colossal cost of £800,000, it was completed in 1757. The dome is built up of variously coloured tiles, an effect of rich elegance being obtained.

E.N.A.

CHICHEN-ITZA, MECCA OF THE ANCIENT MAYANS

Chichen-Itza, in the Mexican province of Yucatan, was the Mecca of the ancient Mayan world. It was founded by the Itzans not later than A.D. 530, and was at its zenith in the twelfth and thirteenth centuries. The Thousand Columns enclose a large plaza surrounded by pyramid-temples, terraces and theatres.

E.N.A.

AN ASTRONOMICAL OBSERVATORY OF THE AZTECS

The Caracol (Spanish for "snail") at Chichen-Itza was an astronomical observatory. A double terrace, reached by stairways, is crowned with a round tower, 75 feet high and 37 feet in diameter. Inside are two circular corridors and a spiral staircase leading to a small chamber for taking observations. It is one of many fine buildings dating from the thirteenth century, when commenced the city's greatest splendour.

F. Crosby

Ewing Galloway

VAST RUINS OF UNKNOWN ORIGIN

Amongst the most mysterious of all the ruins in which Mexico is so rich are those of the great temple at Mitla in the territory of the Zapotecs, in southern Mexico. No one knows their origin, for they differ markedly from either Maya or Toltec buildings. They are remarkable for their decorative designs based obviously on cloth patterns, designs which are paralleled nowhere in the world except in Peru.

STONE PILLARS THAT ARE AGES OLD

The Mitla ruins, which cover a huge area, are extensively decorated with unique geometric sculptures and striking fresco paintings. The great hall inside the temple is now open to the sky, but was originally roofed over by great beams which rested flat upon these lovely stone columns. Built of porphyry, a stone found in some quantity in Mexico, they are a little over 14 feet in height and are most exquisitely proportioned.

Ewing Galloway

SILENT SENTINELS ETERNALLY ASLEEP

The famous silver-mining city of Santa Fé de Guanajuato, capital of a Mexican state of the same name, was founded by the Spaniards in 1554. Today its silver is still mined, but the town is more celebrated for its extensive catacombs built underneath the old Panteon or public cemetery. Here in a stone corridor are arranged, in strange attitudes, long rows of gruesome, mummified bodies of long-departed Spaniards.

Fairchild Aerial Surveys

TAMPICO, MEXICO'S GREATEST OIL PORT

Tampico, on the Gulf of Mexico, the most up-to-date harbour in Mexico, is one of the greatest oil ports in the world. Four of the most productive oil-fields in the country are situated within a hundred miles of it, and sixty-eight pipe-lines centre on it. This picture shows a cluster of steel storage tanks for petroleum.

Ewing Galloway

TOLTEC PYRAMID AND SPANISH CHURCHES

The celebrated Pyramid of Cholula is a man-made mound of adobe (sun-dried brick), the largest of its kind on earth, 204 feet in height with a base 1,000 feet square. Its date is uncertain, but it is ascribed to the Toltecs. A modern church replaces the Temple of Quetzalcoatl that formerly crowned its summit. The pyramid is seen across some of the forty-seven astonishing domes of the Royal Chapel at Cholula.

E.N.A.

SERPENT-HEAD DECORATIONS FOR AN ANCIENT MEXICAN SUN TEMPLE

At San Juan de Teotihuacan, in Mexico, is a collection of impressive monuments to the ancient civilizations which flourished here centuries ago. Chief among them is the Temple of Quetzalcoatl, the golden-haired god of the Toltecs. This picture shows the precipitous stone staircase leading to the top of the temple, which is decorated with the heads of plumed serpents, symbol for the Toltecs of the god of wisdom.

E.N.A.

MEXICO'S FINEST CATHEDRAL

The Cathedral of the Assumption of the Virgin at Mexico City is the principal religious edifice in the country. Begun in 1573 on the site of the temple of Huitzilopochtli, the war-god of the Aztecs, it was consecrated in 1667 and is the finest example of Spanish Renaissance architecture in the New World.

Ewing Galloway

WHERE ONCE A GREAT MAYAN CITY STOOD

In the neighbourhood of Oaxaca City is the extensive Mayan site of Monte Alban, which has not yet been fully excavated but is of a similar nature to that of San Juan Teotihuacan. The ruins above ground crown a level hill-top and comprise remains of temples, fortresses, rock-carvings and dwelling-houses. They represent a remarkable achievement by a race which had nothing but stone implements with which to work.

Ewing Galloway

A STONE THAT RECORDED THE MAYAN CALENDAR

At Quirigua, in Guatemala, are several of the strangely carved sandstone stelae, or pillars, of the ancient Maya peoples, who used to erect them in order to mark the passing of a "katun" (roughly twenty years). The largest of these stelae, seen here, measures 25 feet in height. The calendrical hieroglyphics on the sides have enabled archæologists to establish, with fair accuracy, the chief dates of Mayan history.

E.N.A.

THE CATHEDRAL—CENTRE OF PANAMA CITY

After the destruction of old Panama by Sir Henry Morgan in 1671, the site of the city was removed five miles to the west, where a rocky peninsula projected into the Bay, so offering better prospects of defence than the old site and being nearer the port. A handsome new city was begun in 1673, and the ruins of the strong granite walls that were then erected still stand. This picture shows the splendid cathedral, built in 1760.

Ewing Galloway

CANAL THAT DIVIDES A CONTINENT

Connecting the Atlantic and Pacific Oceans across the narrow isthmus of Panama, the Panama Canal is 50¾ miles in total length. The work was carried out, in the face of enormous difficulties, by the U.S. Corps of Engineers in seven years, and the first ocean steamer passed through on August 3, 1914. The total cost was over £70,000,000. A glance at the map is sufficient to show its commercial importance to the world.

E.N.A.

ON TOP OF THE COPÁN PYRAMID

Copán, the ruined Maya city in Honduras, is buried under vegetation and the alluvial deposits of the Copán River. This picture shows the ruined walls of the room on top of the great pyramid, which is over 200 feet in height and built in the manner of the Egyptian pyramids. The latter, however, served as tombs, whereas the Mayan pyramids were substructures for the temples which crowned them.

New York Times Photos

CHRISTIAN SANCTUARY SET IN A MOUNTAIN GORGE

At Ipiales, a Columbian town near the frontier of Ecuador, is the gleaming white sanctuary of Las Lajas; this gem of neo-Gothic architecture nestles, unexpectedly, in the precipitous ravine of the Rio Carchi. A lofty monumental bridge which has been built over the foaming mountain torrent serves as a processional approach to this celebrated church, which is visited by many thousands of pilgrims annually.

Guss

CHIMBORAZO, GRANDEST OF ECUADOR'S MOUNTAINS

Chimborazo, Ecuador's greatest mountain, is an extinct craterless volcano, one of many, rising among the Cordilleras to a height of 20,428 feet above sea-level. This picture shows its consummate beauty as seen from Riobamba, on the magnificently engineered railway that connects Quito with Guayaquil.

E.N.A.

THE WONDERFUL ROAD AND RAILWAY TO CARACAS

La Guaira, Venezuela's principal seaport, and Caracas, its mountain capital, are united both by a railway and by a modern concrete road. Though the cities are only six miles apart as the crow flies, twenty-three miles of winding railway-track are necessary to overcome the difference in elevation of 2,984 feet. This line, which has been electrified for many years, owes its origin to British capital and enterprise.

E.N.A.

THE INCOMPARABLE MAJESTY OF KAIETEUR FALLS

Situated in the heart of tropical British Guiana, the Kaieteur Falls are amongst the highest of the world's great water-falls, being nearly five times the height of Niagara. The Potaro River, 200 feet deep in the rainy season and nearly 300 feet in width, pours its enormous volume of water over a sheer drop of 741 feet.

E.N.A.

THE "GOLDEN RAILWAY" OF SANTOS

The cable railway from Santos to Alto da Serra is a magnificent piece of engineering, for in a distance of five miles it rises over 2,600 feet. The cost of building it was so great that it has been called the "Golden Railway," but a large proportion of the world's coffee supply travels by this route.

By courtesy of the Brazilian Government

PENHA, THE LOURDES OF BRAZIL

The pilgrimage church at Penha, majestically perched upon a huge escarpment of curiously smooth rock on the outskirts of Rio de Janeiro, dates from the time of the Portuguese ownership of the country and is sometimes known as the Lourdes of Brazil, because of the miracles said to take place there.

Ewing Galloway

AN AERIAL RAILWAY TO THE TOP OF A WORLD-FAMOUS VIEWPOINT

Sugar Loaf Hill or Pão de Assucar, the oddly-shaped mountain that overlooks the harbour of Rio de Janeiro, rises sheer from the sea which washes its base to a height of 1,212 feet. Tourists can now ascend to its summit in nine minutes by means of an aerial ropeway, a change of cars being necessary half-way up.

A FARM WHERE POISONOUS SNAKES ARE REARED

Near São Paulo, the second city of Brazil, is one of the strangest farms in the world, the Instituto Butantan, or Government snake farm. Here, in these curious mud-built hives, poisonous snakes are kept and bred for the sake of their venom, which is extracted to be used as antitoxin for the cure of snake-bite.

E.N.A.

E.N.A.

CHRIST ON THE MOUNTAIN TOP

One of the peaks dominating Rio de Janeiro is the Corcovado or Hunchback Mountain, which is ascended by a rack-and-pinion railway. On its summit, 2,329 feet above the level of the sea, stands a colossal concrete statue of Christ, in a striking attitude of benediction. The height of the figure is 110 feet,

FIVE TORCHES WHICH

A few years before the Second World War an American aerial survey party, operating in the interior of Peru, came unexpectedly upon a phenomenon unique even in a continent of natural wonders. In the Valley of the Volcanoes, branching out from the Andes, were more than forty extinct volcanoes within a distance

New York Times Photos

NO LONGER BURN

of as many miles. This picture shows five craters—a view which can scarcely be matched anywhere else in the world. The close observer will notice well-worn native trails passing across the valley, which indicate that even in this remote region there is a surprising volume of traffic across the mountains,

E.N.A.

HIGHEST STANDARD-GAUGE RAILWAY IN THE WORLD

The one hundred and thirty-seven miles of railway from Callao, the Peruvian seaport, to the mining town of Oroya, were constructed from 1869 onwards by the American engineer, Henry Meiggs, in the face of enormous difficulties. There are sixty-five tunnels and sixty-seven bridges, and the divide is crossed at 15,665 feet. This picture shows a typical scene, the " Bridge of the Little Hell," uniting two tunnels.

Ewing Galloway

E.N.A.

EL MISTI, LOVELY GIANT OF THE ANDES

The city of Arequipa, celebrated for its many quaint old Spanish buildings, stands at an altitude of 7,600 feet, in a beautiful valley at the foot of El Misti. The latter is a quiescent volcano, with a symmetrical cone of exquisite beauty, capped with everlasting snow, and its height of 20,013 feet makes it one of the highest peaks of the Andes.

RESTING PLACE OF A GREAT CONQUISTADOR

Facing the Plaza de Armas, or main square, of Lima, the Peruvian capital, is one of the finest cathedrals of Spanish America. Francisco Pizarro, conqueror of the Incas, laid its foundation stone on January 18, 1535—the very day of the founding of the city. It was consecrated in 1625, and after his death Pizarro's remains were laid to rest there.

E.N.A.

THE IMMENSE PRE-INCA RUINS OF CHAN CHAN

On the Peruvian coast are the remains of the vast city of Chan Chan, capital of the Chimu people, who were exterminated by the Incas about the year 1400. Its walls, 30 to 40 feet high and 8 to 12 feet thick, are constructed of adobe (sun-dried clay), but they have survived owing to the rainlessness of the district.

Ewing Galloway

THE BEAUTIFUL STONEWORK OF MACHU PICCHU

Machu Picchu, one of the most famous retreats of the Incas, situated some 7,000 feet up in the Andes, has been excavated by the National Geographic Society of the United States, in conjunction with Yale University. The Incas were famous for the meticulous way in which they prepared the stonework for their buildings, and this picture shows the remains of the Great Tower, with its beautifully cut and fitted masonry.

E.N.A.

A DOMINICAN CONVENT ONCE AN INCA TEMPLE

Founded by Manco Capac, first of the Incas, about the eleventh century, Cuzco, 11,380 feet above sea-level, was the capital of the Inca Empire until its capture by Pizarro in 1533, and it contains numerous relics of Incan architecture. The Convent of Santo Domingo, a sixteenth-century foundation, is built upon the remains of the Inca Temple of the Sun, or Curicancha, a famous masterpiece of stonework.

E.N.A.

A GIGANTIC INCA WALL

Cuzco is a curious mixture of massive Inca structures, early Spanish buildings, and crude huts of adobe or sun-dried brick. This narrow street is typical. It is lined by a section of the famous Inca wall in the Calle Jon de Loreto, which is constructed of huge blocks of stone, perfectly cut and fitted together without the use of cement, but nowadays the stones carry telephone wires and modern electric lights on their face.

New York Times Photo

WHERE THE ANCIENTS GATHERED

The Maras pampas lie about fifteen miles to the north-west of Cuzco. Aerial survey has revealed a group of amphitheatres which seem to have been overlooked by archæologists on the ground. Worship of clan gods is characteristic of the Inca period, and although no mention of these "Yale bowls" has been found in the literature of the region, it is possible that they were used for religious presentations.

E.N.A.

THE GATE OF THE SUN AT TIAHUANACO

Close to Lake Titicaca lie the remains of the very ancient metropolis of Tiahuanaco, with its extensive stone ruins of the early civilization from which probably sprang the founders of the Inca empire. Of the origin of these ruins nothing is known, but they are quite unlike Inca structures. This picture shows all that is left of the Gate of the Sun, or Ak-Kapana, with its striking relief-decoration of unique pattern.

Photos: E.N.A.

RUINS OVER TWELVE THOUSAND YEARS OLD

Among the famous ruins of Tiahuanaco the most impressive remains are the colossal blocks of stone, now overthrown, but believed to have once formed the throne of the ruler of some mysterious pre-Inca people. Their age is estimated at between 12,000 and 14,000 years. The whole site is a marvel of building.

PREHISTORIC IDOL

One of the stone wonders of Tiahuanaco is this extraordinary head of some prehistoric deity, excavated near the shore of Lake Titicaca. How this prehistoric people, ignorant of iron, were able to acquire such skill in stone-cutting remains an inscrutable mystery. Certainly, such works in stone are among the finest achievements of primitive man.

E.N.A.

A SKYSCRAPER OF SOUTH AMERICA

Montevideo, the Uruguayan capital and seaport, is a well-built modern city of three-quarters of a million inhabitants. The Palacio Salvo, seen here, is the highest concrete structure in the world and the tallest building in South America. Twelve storeys high, with a fourteen-storey tower superimposed, the Salvo Building is over 275 feet in height and is the most conspicuous landmark of this rapidly expanding city.

E.N.A.

FINEST OF URUGUAY'S RAILWAY BRIDGES

Near Salto, the third city of Uruguay, is this magnificent steel-and-concrete bridge of the state railway. Much livestock destined for Europe passes over it on the way to the port. The bridge spans the Dayman River, which in the rainy seasons expands from a marsh to a rushing stream hundreds of feet wide.

E.N.A.

THE WORLD'S MOST BEAUTIFUL PARK

Buenos Aires, with two-and-a-half million inhabitants, is the largest city in the southern hemisphere. The Parque 3 de Febrero, in the suburb of Palermo, is claimed as the world's most beautiful park. Its avenues form a magnificent promenade, and one portion is set aside as a zoological garden, with a large collection of animals and birds. The number and variety of its plants and trees are without parallel.

Ewing Galloway

ARGENTINA'S CAPITOL AND NATIONAL MONUMENT

The Palacio del Congreso in Buenos Aires, a building of vast size, crowned by a splendid dome, is the seat of the legislature of Argentina and the meeting-place of the Senate and the Chamber of Deputies. In front of it stands the Argentine National Monument, an ornate structure of stone and bronze. Buenos Aires is a city of fine buildings, annual prizes encouraging a high standard of architecture.

G.P.A.

A WONDER OF THE ANDES—THE INCA'S BRIDGE

This remarkable rock bridge, known as the Puente del Inca, or Inca's Bridge, has been formed high up in the Andes Mountains some 9,000 feet above sea-level. It is, of course, a product of Nature and not a man-made Inca construction, and has been cut by the Mendoza River in the course of countless centuries.

Ewing Galloway

THE CHRIST OF THE ANDES—PLEDGE OF PEACE BETWEEN TWO NATIONS

Where the old road over the Andes crosses the frontier, there stands a huge bronze statue of Christ with these words carved on its base: " Sooner shall these mountains crumble into dust than the peoples of Argentina and Chile break the peace which they have sworn to maintain at the feet of Christ the Redeemer."

Ewing Galloway

SUBLIME MAJESTY OF ACONCAGUA

Rising to a height of 23,000 feet above the level of the sea, Aconcagua is always considered the monarch of the Andes and is, in fact, the highest peak anywhere in the world outside the Himalayas. It fully deserves the pride of place accorded it as the most grandiose of all the magnificent Andean peaks.

D. McLeish

THE WORLD'S MOST CELEBRATED GATEWAY—ENTRANCE TO THE KARNAK TEMPLES

The entrance to the precincts enclosing the famous temple-ruins of Karnak is by a magnificent sandstone portal erected by the Egyptian Pharaoh, Euergetes I (246–222 B.C.), the third Ptolemy. The reliefs show the king praying and sacrificing to the gods. Under the cornice is a winged sun, emblem of Horus, which was placed over temple gateways to avert evil. The austere beauty of the gateway is most striking.

AFRICA

THIRD in size among the continents of the world, Africa, 11,500,000 square miles in area, is the most sparsely populated of them all with the exception of Oceania. The continent is surrounded by water on all sides, for across that minute triangle of land known as the Sinai Peninsula, which forms a land bridge between Africa and Asia, has been cut the Suez Canal, one of the great feats of world engineering. Let us take a glance at some of the wonders to be found in this mighty continent.

The Barbary States—Morocco, divided between a French and a Spanish protectorate; Algeria, now an integral part of France; and Tunisia, a French protectorate—are mainly inhabited by Berbers, indigenous peoples of various types. The regions north-west of the great mountain backbone, the Atlas, are richly fertile, though lacking in trees and forests, and attract lovers of the picturesque.

Little remains of Rome's formidable rival, Carthage, but here are to be seen the most magnificent series of ruined Roman cities in the world. Such individual buildings as the theatre of Timgad, the prætorium of Lambessa, the temple at Dougga, the amphitheatre of El Djem, the aqueduct at New Carthage, are merely a few examples of the endless store of splendid late-Roman constructions that North Africa has to show. Byzantines, represented by the basilica of Tebessa, were followed by Vandals; and then came a great wave of Arab conquerors, who marked North Africa with a permanent stamp and gave it the religion of Islam in its most fanatical form. Few regions of the Mohammedan world can boast a finer series of mosques and minarets than the Hassan Tower of Rabat, the Kutubiya Mosque of Marrakesh, the Kairwan Mosque at Fez, the ruined tower of Mansura, the Great Mosque at that most Arab of all Arab cities, Kairouan.

The most Saharan in character of the countries of North Africa are Tripolitania, which has as its capital the beautiful walled city of Tripoli, set amid a million date palms, and Cyrenaica, once the seat of a flourishing Greek colony. Here are to be found the newly excavated ruins of Leptis Magna, once the greatest city in the African continent.

Egypt, the north-eastern corner of Africa, has been well described as " the gift of the Nile." For were it not for that river, and the silt it carries down from the Abyssinian highlands, Egypt would be wholly (as two-thirds of it actually is) an empty desert. The Nile flows for its last thousand miles through the length of the country, and its annual overflow, regulated by those epic creations of modern engineering, the Aswan and Asiut barrages, enables the hard-working fellahin to produce as many as three crops a year.

THE VALLEY OF THE KINGS

Here we find some of the most colossal buildings in human history: pyramids, consummate in their mastery of mathematical engineering; temples, some of them remarkable for their dignified simplicity, and others gigantic in size and so elaborate as to appear clumsy and ostentatious in design. No other country can show such a wealth of statuary, from the colossal figures of Memnon and Rameses to the tiny tomb figures of Osiris, Isis and Horus, without including those mysterious sphinxes at Thebes, Karnak, Luxor and elsewhere; such splendid obelisks as those of Heliopolis and Alexandria; such columns and pylons as those of Karnak and Luxor, of Dendera, Abydos and Philae, of Medinat Habu, Deir-el-Bahri, Abu Simbel; such labyrinthine rock-hewn burial places as those in the Valley of the Kings.

South of the Saharan regions and of Egypt lies the Sudan, the " Country of the Blacks." That portion which lies south of Egypt is known as the Anglo-Egyptian Sudan and is under the joint sovereignty of Great Britain and Egypt. The Gezira, or triangular area between the two branches, is celebrated for the wonderful crops of cotton and grain which, thanks to the Sennar Dam, can be grown there.

Abyssinia is the home of a primitive Christianity of Coptic type, introduced as early as the fourth century. Its picturesque inhabitants and grand mountain scenery make it one of the world's most interesting lands. At Aksum there are strange obelisks and altar tombs of early date.

South of the Barbary States, across the whole width of the continent, there stretches the world's greatest desert. The western part,

E.N.A.

A MINARET SEVEN HUNDRED YEARS OLD

At Rabat, on the west coast, once known as the "Key of Morocco," and a junction of many caravan routes, stands the beautiful Tower of Hassan, built in 1197, according to tradition, and 145 feet high. The broken columns are all that remains of the mosque to which it was once attached as a minaret.

with a thousand-mile frontage on the Atlantic, forms the famous Sahara.

The interior of this part of Africa forms French West Africa, a colonial dominion more than eight times as extensive as the mother country, stretching from Algeria and Morocco to the Gulf of Guinea, and from the Atlantic to Lake Chad. It is divided up into various colonies: Senegal, French Guinea, Ivory Coast, Dahomey, French Sudan and others. Interspersed among these French possessions, and all with a seaboard on the Atlantic, are Gambia, Sierra Leone, Gold Coast and Nigeria (these all British colonies), besides Portuguese Guinea and Liberia, a Negro republic ruled by descendants of freed American slaves. The Cameroons, taking their name from a great volcano which rises direct from the sea-coast, were formerly a German colony but are now divided as trusteeship territory between Britain and France.

The most prominent physical feature of Central Africa is the basin of the Congo, that great river associated for ever with Stanley's name and unsurpassed for volume save by the Amazon alone.

Practically the whole of the Congo basin is contained politically in the Belgian Congo. It includes the wonderful province of Katanga, in the south-east, where are those masterpieces of nature, the Stanley Falls, on the Congo, and the Kalula Falls on the Lualaba, its upper stream.

The eastern part of Africa's equatorial zone, East Africa, is in British occupation, divided between Kenya Colony, Uganda Protectorate and the trusteeship territory of Tanganyika (the former German East Africa). Here African scenery is at its grandest. Kilimanjaro, Kenya, Ruwenzori, Elgon and the rest, the highest mountains in the continent, are all extinct volcanoes. Here, too, is the region of the great lakes—Victoria, Albert, Edward, Tanganyika, Rudolf and the others.

BURIAL PLACE OF RHODES

Rhodesia, comprising two British territories, Northern and Southern, is the creation of Cecil Rhodes and his British South Africa Company. Rhodes chose as his burial place the country he loved so well, and among the great rounded boulders of the Matopo Hills, within sight of the " View of the World," is the tombstone of the great empire-builder. On the Tanganyika boundary are the Kalambo Falls, the second highest in the world (880 feet in a single leap), but these are far surpassed in sublimity by the world-famous Victoria Falls.

In Rhodesia is found Africa's most mysterious ruin, Zimbabwe, whose walls and temples and conical towers, all achieved without a vestige of mortar, but with an enormous expenditure of materials and labour, are a most unexpected sight. The Birchenough Road Bridge over the Sabi river and the Victoria Falls railway bridge are first-rate engineering achievements, but they pale into insignificance beside the longest bridge in the world—built over the Lower Zambezi.

A WEALTHY LAND

Finally we come to the Union of South Africa, whose area exceeds that of Great Britain, France and Germany combined.

Cape Town, the threshold of South Africa, enjoys one of the mildest and healthiest climates known to man, and " in all the world there is no city so beautifully situated," with the monumental pile of Table Mountain towering in the background.

Named by Vasco da Gama after the Christmas Day on which he first sighted it, Natal is the " Garden Colony," rising in terraces to its magnificent natural frontier, the Drakensberg, a vast land of rocky peaks and escarpments, of profound gorges whence great rivers issue to the plains. It is a land, too, of fine waterfalls.

The Karroo, continued northwards into the Orange Free State, supports vast flocks of sheep on its flowery pastures. Transvaal, too, first settled in the " Great Trek " of the Dutch pioneers, is mainly a prairie land. In fact, agriculture and cattle-raising are the real strength of the Union, in spite of the dazzling wealth in diamonds and gold exported from Kimberley and the Rand around Johannesburg.

The Kimberley Mine, with " the greatest hole on earth," and the Premier Mine at Pretoria, have produced an almost embarrassing quantity of diamonds, but even their value is small compared with the annual £75,000,000 worth of gold dug out from that Eldorado, the Witwatersrand. Johannesburg grows rapidly and now contains one-sixth of the white population of the Union.

Africa, as this survey shows, is a land of staggering contrasts which make the continent a storehouse of amazing wonders.

E.N.A.

CRAG-BUILT CITY SACRED TO THE MOORS

Mulai Idris, who died in A.D. 791, was the Sultan who introduced Mahommedanism into Morocco, and he is consequently venerated as the country's greatest saint. The whole town of Mulai Idris, Zarhon, the scene of his death, is considered as a sanctuary. Its chief claim to distinction, however, is its remarkable site. The town has been built completely over a huge rock crag which rises sheer from the floor of a valley.

E.N.A.

A MOSQUE TOWER OVER 200 FEET HIGH

Marrakesh, or Morocco City, is the southern capital of Morocco and one of its largest cities. Its principal place of worship is the Kutubiya Mosque, which was built in the twelfth century and is considered to be one of the leading examples of its period. Its beautifully decorated brick minaret is 215 feet in height.

E.N.A.

AN OPEN-AIR THEATRE FOR ANCIENT ROME'S COLONISTS

Timgad, once a flourishing Roman colony in North Africa, founded in A.D. 100 by order of the Emperor Trajan, was destroyed by the Berbers in 535. Among the most striking of its excavated remains is the theatre, cut out of a hill-side. The auditorium, 70 yards wide, could accommodate 4,000 spectators.

E.N.A.

RESIDENCE OF A LONG-DEAD MILITARY GOVERNOR

The grandest Roman ruin in Algeria—and, in fact, the sole surviving building of its kind—is the Praetorium, or residence of the military commander, at Lambessa, the centre of the Roman power in Numidia and headquarters of the Third Legion. The building shown here was the entrance-gateway to the praetorium.

Ewing Galloway

AN ANCIENT PYRAMID—CELEBRATED LANDMARK OF THE ALGERIAN COAST

A prominent seamark on the Algerian coast is the gigantic stone Tomb of the Christian Woman, so called from the crosses on the door panels. In reality it was a tomb erected by King Juba II of Mauretania at the beginning of the Christian era. The base measures 70 yards each way, and the height is 108 feet.

E.N.A.

A STRIKING RELIC OF ANCIENT CARTHAGE

Proud Carthage, once the Queen of the Seas and Rome's formidable adversary in three great wars, was razed to the ground after her final defeat by Scipio Africanus in 146 B.C., and very little of the ancient city is now visible. Perhaps the most striking relics are these cisterns, part of the city's original reservoirs, consisting of seventeen great barrel-vaults, which are still used as part of Tunis's water-supply system.

E.N.A.

GRACEFUL PORTICO OF DOUGGA'S MAGNIFICENT TEMPLE

The Capitol, or Temple of Jupiter, Juno and Minerva, at Dougga is the finest Roman temple in Tunisia. The portico, shown here, consists of six Corinthian columns in limestone, 43 feet high. Two citizens of Thugga founded it in the reign of Marcus Aurelius (A.D. 161–180). During the Byzantine period the temple, on its commanding site, served as a fortress. Despite ill-usage its remains are well preserved.

Mondiale

THE STRANGE GRANARIES OF MEDENINE

Medenine is situated in a Saharan oasis, near the Tripolitanian frontier. Here are to be seen these remarkable four-storey store-houses and granaries, now disused and ruinous, some of them cut in the hill-side. Access to them is partly by means of staircases of dried mud and partly by projecting stepping-stones.

E.N.A.

ROME'S GRANDEST RELIC IN NORTH AFRICA

The most impressive Roman structure in the whole of North Africa is the Amphitheatre at El-Djem, which was once the thriving city of Thysdrus. Built in the third century A.D., it is oval in shape, with axes of 163 and 133 yards. The top storey has long disappeared, and the bottom one is buried 10 feet deep. In the heyday of the Roman Empire, it possessed only four amphitheatres larger than this.

Ewing Galloway

THE MARVELLOUS AQUEDUCT OF CARTHAGE

This magnificent aqueduct once supplied water to Colonia Julia Carthago, the Roman city that took the place of ancient Carthage. Begun in A.D. 117, during the reign of the Emperor Hadrian, it was not completed till A.D. 161, and it represents a colossal feat of engineering. Over 7½ miles of it still survive intact.

Lubinski

A MODERN MOSQUE AT KAIROUAN

The Arab town of Kairouan, "one of the four gates of Paradise," formerly forbidden to unbelievers, was once the religious centre of North Africa. The remarkable Scimitar Mosque, seen here, in spite of its medieval appearance, was built in the nineteenth century by a saint called Amor Abeda, entirely out of alms collected for the purpose. Its five characteristic domes and its solid masonry are noteworthy.

E.N.A.

THE GREAT MOSQUE OF KAIROUAN—ONE OF ISLAM'S HOLY PLACES

The Great, or Sidi Okba, Mosque at Kairouan ranks as the fourth greatest sanctuary of Islam, after the mosques of Mecca, Medina and Jerusalem. Founded in A.D. 671, it is mainly a work of the ninth century. The minaret is 128 feet in height; its fortress-like lower portion dates back to A.D. 724. This mosque contains some famous examples of Mohammedan wood-carving as much as a thousand years old.

E.N.A.

A FOREST OF COLUMNS IN KAIROUAN'S GREAT MOSQUE

The Great Mosque of Kairouan is an immense building, measuring 438 by 240 feet and covering an area of 2¼ acres. It is composed of six aisles with eight rows of columns, the shafts of which, removed from ancient buildings, are of marble, onyx, granite, porphyry and other stones, while the capitals are of Roman, early Christian, Byzantine and Punic types. The clumsy braces and stucco decoration are more modern.

F. Henle

ONCE THE GREATEST ROMAN COLONY IN ALL AFRICA

The greatest of the Roman settlements in North Africa was Leptis Magna, the vast ruins of which are near Tripoli. Both the harbour and the once thriving city were for long completely buried, but the grand ruins, dating from the reign of the Emperor Septimius Severus (A.D. 193–211), have now been largely excavated, in excellent preservation thanks to the protection afforded by the sand which covered them.

AMONGST THE GREATEST WONDERS OF

The Pyramids of Giza are the most imposing of the six groups of pyramids that stand on the edge of the desert in the vicinity of Cairo. On the left of this picture is the Great Pyramid, or Pyramid of Cheops, the largest of all, built nearly five thousand years ago. The sides, each 746 feet long, face the points of the compass; its height is 450 feet; the area covered is nearly 13 acres. Some idea of the enormous amount

Fox

THE ANCIENT AND THE MODERN WORLD

of labour involved may be gained from the statement that it consists of 2,300,000 blocks of stone, averaging about 2½ tons each. The Second Pyramid, that of Chephren, is only slightly smaller, but the Third, of Mykerinos, is about half the size. In the foreground is set out the Cemetery, with the tombs of members of the royal household and high officials. In the distance are seen other and smaller pyramids.

E.N.A.

D. McLeish

ONE OF EGYPT'S OLDEST TEMPLES

Situated in the shade of the Great Pyramid is the Temple of Nefru, of particular interest because it is probably the oldest yet discovered in this land of temples, dating as far back as the second dynasty (5000 B.C.). Though overshadowed in size by the tremendous creations of later ages, its simple dignity and unimpeachable proportions are none the less effective.

AN OBELISK FOUR THOUSAND YEARS OLD

Sole relic of the famous Temple of the Sun-God Ra at Heliopolis is this obelisk of red granite, 66 feet in height, and dating from about 1950 B.C. The inscription (which is the same on all four sides) reads: " Sesostris I, King of Upper and Lower Egypt, Lord of the Diadems and Son of the Sun, whom the divine spirits of On (i.e., Heliopolis) love, erected this obelisk in celebration of a jubilee."

D. McLeish

POMPEY'S PILLAR—A FAMOUS LANDMARK AT ALEXANDRIA

Pompey's Pillar at Alexandria certainly does not mark the tomb of Pompey, as was once supposed, but may have been a column from the Temple of Serapis, erected here by the Byzantine Emperor Theodosius to commemorate the destruction of that pagan temple. Of red granite, it is 88 feet high and 9 feet in diameter. The sphinx which stands before it was possibly brought from the temple of Heliopolis.

E.N.A.

PICTURESQUE WALLS AND MINARETS OF CAIRO'S FORTRESS

The Citadel which commands Cairo was originally built in the twelfth century by the great Saladin (famous in the Crusades) with stones from the Pyramids of Giza. Within its precincts stands the conspicuous yellow Alabaster Mosque, built by Mohammed Ali, Governor of Egypt, and completed in 1857; it was in this fortress that he treacherously massacred his allies the Mamelukes, 470 in all, in 1811.

E.N.A.

GORGEOUS INTERIOR OF THE ALABASTER MOSQUE

Mohammed Ali's Mosque in the Citadel of Cairo is very impressive in its dimensions and lighting. The walls and columns are of yellow alabaster, and there are innumerable glass lamps. In the centre is the pulpit, and on the left the reading desk. Mohammed Ali, who died in 1849, was buried here. The mosque contains a well traditionally known as Joseph's Well, sunk through the rock to Nile level.

D. McLeish

THE SUPERB TOMBS OF THE MAMELUKE SULTANS

Outside the walls of Cairo are the tombs of the Mamelukes, an unsurpassed group of twelve tomb-mosques built by the Circassian Mameluke sultans of Egypt. The finest are those of Barquq, who died in 1399, founder of the dynasty, and Qait Bey, who died in 1496. At one time they fell into sad disrepair, but they have now been restored by the Government. Three of the tombs are seen in this picture.

D. McLeish

THE GRANDEST EXAMPLE OF ARAB ARCHITECTURE IN EGYPT

Among the innumerable mosques of Cairo, the finest is undoubtedly the Sultan Hasan Mosque, built in 1356–1363. The buildings, which include a "madrasa" or theological college, cover an area of 85,000 square feet; the dome is 180 feet high, and the south minaret (the tallest in Cairo) 285 feet.

THE SPHINX—ANCIENT SYMBOL OF MAJESTY

One of the most famous of world wonders is the sphinx which guards the Second Pyramid. This immense figure of a lion with a king's head, 240 feet long and 66 feet high, was sculptured out of a huge mass of rock found in a stone quarry. Ascribed to the period of the fourth Egyptian dynasty, between 4800 and 4500 B.C., it was probably built by Chephren, who erected the pyramid seen behind. Originally, the sphinx was covered with lime-wash and painted.

SPHINXES AT KARNAK

Each of the various temples at Karnak is approached by a processional avenue of sphinxes. In the case of Thebes (of which Karnak forms a part) the sphinx-figures are those of recumbent rams, that animal being sacred to the local god Amun. The avenue in this picture, leading to the Temple of Khons, was set up by Rameses XI in the eleventh century before Christ.

E.N.A.

D. McLeish

D. McLeish

GIGANTIC COLUMNS OF THE TEMPLE OF AMUN

The Great Hypostyle Hall of the Temple of Amun at Karnak, built by Rameses I and his successor, Seti I, about 1300 B.C., is a highlight of ancient Egyptian architecture. It covers an area of 6,000 square yards, and each of the immense sandstone columns seen in this picture is decorated with painted reliefs and inscriptions. Each column measures nearly 12 feet in diameter and 70 feet in height.

E.N.A.

AN EGYPTIAN TEMPLE ONCE USED AS A CHURCH

At Medinet Habu, near Thebes, is the Temple of Rameses III, dating from about 1198 to 1167 B.C. The temple was originally dedicated to the local god Amun, but its magnificent Second Court, shown here, measuring 138 feet by 125, was later used as a Christian church. On the south side are round columns with lotus-bud capitals; on the west, rectangular pillars with figures of the King represented as Osiris.

E.N.A.

ALL THAT REMAINS OF EGYPT'S LARGEST STATUE

The Ramesseum, or Mortuary Temple of Rameses II (about 1292–1225 B.C.), at Thebes, is unfortunately in a bad state of preservation. On the right of this picture are fragments of one of the largest statues erected in Egypt, a Colossus of Rameses, to which Shelley wrote a sonnet. When perfect it was over 57 feet in height, and weighed 1,000 tons. The figures still standing are Osiride statues.

D. McLeish

DILAPIDATED BUT WORLD FAMOUS—THE COLOSSI OF MEMNON

The Colossi of Memnon, which date from the fourteenth century B.C., form a prominent landmark on the west bank of the Nile near Thebes. They really commemorate Amenophis III, who was the Memnon celebrated by the Greeks as a hero of the Trojan war. The two statues are each 64 feet in height. That on the left is the celebrated "Vocal" Memnon which used to emit a musical note at sunrise.

E.N.A.

A ROCK-HEWN TEMPLE BUILT BY A FAMOUS QUEEN

The white terraced walls of the Great Temple of Amun at Deir-el-Bahri, near Thebes, stand out in brilliant prominence against the precipices of golden rock. The temple was built by Queen Hatshepsut, who was wife and co-ruler of Thothmes III. In the rocks behind the temple, in 1881, were discovered seventeen mummies, including that of Rameses II. At one period the temple served as a Christian monastery.

E.N.A.

WHERE THE TUTANKHAMUN TREASURES WERE FOUND

In the Valley of the Kings, near Thebes, are sixty-one rock-tombs of the eighteenth, nineteenth and twentieth dynasties of Egyptian monarchs. This picture shows the entrance to the famous tomb of Tutankhamun, who died about the year 1350 B.C. Its contents are now in the Cairo Museum.

E.N.A.

A BEAUTIFUL SURVIVAL OF LATE EGYPTIAN ART

The Temple of Hathor at Denderá, seen in the background of this picture, is a famous example of the architecture of the Ptolemies, commenced in the first century B.C. and completed under Augustus. The gateway and much of the decorative work date from a later period. The sandstone temple and other buildings stand within a vast brick enclosure nearly 300 yards square. They are marvellously preserved. The six columns of the vestibule are adorned with heads of Hathor, the goddess of love.

D. McLeish.

AFTER TWO THOUSAND YEARS

The Temple of Horus, the Sun God, at Edfu, is in a better state of preservation than any other building of comparable antiquity in Egypt. It was begun in 237 B.C. by Ptolemy Euergetes I, and completed by 57 B.C. The reliefs on the Pylon, whose western tower is seen in this picture, illustrate kings praying and offering sacrifice to Horus and other deities. The size of the columns can be gauged from the figure on the right. Although comparatively recent, it has many features of older Egyptian architecture.

CONTRAST IN COLUMNS AT

The colonnades of the Temple of Luxor, at Thebes, are among the grandest relics of ancient Egypt. The contrast between the simple columns on the right and the clustered papyrus columns on the left, each more than 50 feet in height, is very effective. The temple, which measures 853 feet in length and 181 feet in breadth, was built by Amenophis III, the Memnon of the Greeks, who reigned from about 1411

E.N.A.

THE GREAT TEMPLE OF LUXOR

to 1375 B.C. Rameses II, the greatest builder among the Pharaohs, enlarged it. The temple was dedicated to the Egyptian god Amun, to his wife Mut, and to their son Khons, the Moon God. At a subsequent period it was converted into a church, and it still retains a small mosque within its precincts. The Luxor Obelisk which stands in the centre of the Place de la Concorde, Paris, came from this ancient temple.

W.G.W.—K

J. I. F. Knight

THE HISTORIC SPHINX OF MEMPHIS

In the picturesque palm grove surrounding the village of Saqqara lies a magnificent sphinx of alabaster, with the features of Rameses II. Excavated in 1912, it measures 26 feet in length and 14 feet in height, and its weight is estimated at 80 tons. Close by is the site of Memphis, once the capital of Egypt.

E.N.A.

THE EARLIEST FORM OF THE PYRAMID

The famous Step-Pyramid of Saqqara was built as a tomb monument by King Zoser, of the third dynasty, about 2700 B.C., and is the earliest important building in Egypt. Rectangular in plan (413 feet by 344), it measures 200 feet in height and is composed of limestone blocks. Beneath it is a series of chambers. Zoser was a great builder, and appears to have been one of the most powerful of the early Pharaohs.

E.N.A.

A TRIUMPH OF CARVING—THE BAS RELIEFS OF SAQQARA

Saqqara is one vast necropolis, with numerous tombs of many periods. One of the most famous is the Mastaba of Ti, a high official of the fifth dynasty (about 2500 B.C.). The splendidly preserved mural reliefs, which it contains in great profusion, are among the finest existing examples of ancient art.

W. F. Taylor

THE ROCK-HEWN COLOSSI OF ABU SIMBEL

The two rock temples of Abu Simbel, in the extreme south of Egypt, are stupendous monuments of Egyptian architecture. At the entrance, hewn out of the cliff, are colossal figures of Rameses II, each of which is 65 feet in height. Note the mild expression and characteristic nose of this Pharaoh of the Israelitish oppression, who wears the double crown symbolical of the union of Upper and Lower Egypt.

E.N.A.

PILLARED HALL OF A GREAT TEMPLE

At the ancient city of Abydos stands the wonderful Temple of Seti I, commenced about 1300 B.C. by that king and completed by the inveterate temple-builder, Rameses II. The material is a limestone of peculiar durability. The roof of the Second Hypostyle Hall, illustrated above, is supported by a number of beautiful columns, some with papyrus-bud capitals (right) and others unadorned (left).

E.N.A.

THE UNDER-WATER TEMPLES OF PHILAE

The island of Philae, world famed for its beauty, has now been unfortunately submerged by the construction of the Nile dam. Its temples, however, are still accessible when the river level is low. On the left of this picture is the Temple of Isis, with its magnificent pylons, begun by Ptolemy Philadelphus and finished by Euergetes I (third century B.C.). On the right is the exquisite kiosk, of Roman construction.

Mondiale

SENNAR DAM, BASIS OF A VAST IRRIGATION SCHEME

Constructed by the British Government in 1921–1925, the Sennar Dam, south of Khartoum, is one of the greatest barrages in the world, providing water for the irrigation of the corn and cotton fields in an enormous area of the Gezira province in the Sudan. It measures 9,240 feet in length and 107 feet in height.

E.N.A.

A MARSH ALMOST AS LARGE AS ENGLAND

One of Africa's greatest natural wonders is the Sudd, an enormous expanse of swamp in southern Sudan, covering an area one-third the size of the British Isles. The Albert Nile, or Bahr-el-Jebel, flows through it for 470 miles and navigation on it is frequently obstructed by floating masses of papyrus and other water plants. This picture shows Nile steamers forcing their way through a typical stretch of the Sudd.

E.N.A.

THE STRANGE OBELISKS OF AKSUM

At Aksum, the sacred city of the Ethiopians, are a number of carved and ornamented stelae, or stone pillars, of lofty dimensions, varying from 50 to 100 feet in height, each with an altar at its foot. They are probably tombstones erected in the fourth century A.D. by the Semitic conquerors of Abyssinia.

Photos: E.N.A.

THE MAGNIFICENT FALLS OF THE BLUE NILE

The greatest eastern tributary of the White Nile (the main stream) is the Blue Nile, which joins it at Khartoum. The Blue Nile or Abai, rising in the Gojam Highlands of Abyssinia, flows through Lake Tsana and then rushes through a long series of cataracts, descending 4,000 feet before leaving Abyssinia. The greatest of these waterfalls are the East Falls, near Dildi, not far from the outlet of Lake Tsana.

STRANGE MINARET OF AN ANCIENT MOSQUE

Mukdishu, " the Immense " (as the Arabs call it), was one of the chief cities of the Zenj (Zanzibar) Empire established by Arabs and Persians on the east coast of Africa in the eleventh century. Its famous mosque, built in 1180, is the oldest in the country, and has a squat minaret of unusually massive form.

Mondiale

TIMBUKTU—" MEETING POINT OF CAMEL AND CANOE "

Situated on the southern verge of the Sahara, close to the River Niger, the famous city of Timbuktu, celebrated in romance and legend, is in reality a sun-baked cosmopolitan town consisting of flat-roofed earthen houses and mosques. At one time it was the capital of a great negro empire and the chief trading centre of the south-western Sahara and the Sudan, where Arab and Negro traders gathered.

E.N.A.

THE DWELLINGS OF RÉHÉ—QUAINTEST OF NEGRO TOWNSHIPS

French Sudan comprises a great plateau of granite and limestone in the upper basin of the River Niger. Amongst the most astonishing of its sights is Réhé (shown here) nestling for protection under its great cliff, one of the most extraordinary native townships in all Africa. Its houses, built closely together, made principally of dried mud and each curiously tower-like in construction, are all thatched with straw.

A QUEER CORN-BIN

Dahomey is one of the French West African group of colonies, with a coastline (formerly known as the Slave Coast) on the Gulf of Guinea. The earthen corn-bin shown here is peculiar to the Konkombwa people of Tschopowa and forms an efficient protection against fire, rats and other vermin. Filled from the top, it holds several tons of grain.

MAGNIFICENT FALLS IN THE HEART OF THE JUNGLE

In the remote south-eastern corner of the Belgian Congo, not far from the important town of Bukama, the limit of navigation, are the superb Kalula Falls on the headwaters of the River Lualaba, one of the principal affluents of the Congo. In a magnificent setting of equatorial jungle, these waterfalls are over 150 feet in height.

E.N.A.

E.N.A.

CRACK IN THE EARTH'S CRUST 4,000 MILES LONG

One of the most staggering of natural phenomena in the world is the Great Rift Valley, the course of which geographers have traced for over 4,000 miles, in fact from the Jordan Valley southwards through the Red Sea, Abyssinia and East Africa to Lake Nyasa. This view shows part of the eastern Rift Valley in Kenya, the prospect from the top of the Elgeyo escarpment, 8,000 feet above the valley floor.

A SKYSCRAPER BUILT BY INSECTS

Termites, wrongly called white ants, for they are more closely related to grasshoppers than to ants, are social insects common in the tropics. A queen termite may lay 100,000,000 eggs and their skyscraper nests sometimes attain a height of 20 feet. This picture shows a typical termite city built beside the arterial motor road which runs across Uganda.

RIPON FALLS—SOURCE OF THE WHITE NILE

On the northern shore of Victoria Nyanza, near Jinja, are the magnificent Ripon Falls, which are considered to be the source of the Nile; for they mark the exit of the river from the great lake. Some 17,657 cubic feet of water pour over the rocks every second, and the river descends 700 feet in a succession of rapids throughout the next 50 miles.

Photos : E.N.A.

Nyasaland Railways Ltd.

A RAILWAY BRIDGE OVER TWO MILES LONG

Fourth in size of the rivers of Africa, the great River Zambezi is crossed near Sena, in Mozambique, by a magnificent bridge which carries the railway from Beira to Blantyre in Nyasaland. Completed in 1935 after 4½ years' labour, this 46-span bridge is 12,064 feet long and cost a million and a half pounds. Nearly 16,000 tons of steelwork was used in this triumph of British engineering design and construction.

E.N.A.

A "MIRACLE" OF AFRICA'S GREATEST LAKE

Lake Victoria, situated between Kenya, Tanganyika and Uganda, is, with the exception of Lake Superior, the largest freshwater lake in the world. It has an area of 26,828 square miles, its total length is about 255 miles, and its width about 155 miles. The lake was discovered by Captain Speke in 1858.

E.N.A.

FLOATING ISLANDS THAT APPEAR AND DISAPPEAR

One of the most astonishing of all natural phenomena is to be found in the "floating islands" on Lake Victoria. The top picture of the Bismarck Rocks, near Muanza in Tanganyika, was taken five minutes before the picture below. A vast floating island of matted papyrus and other water plants had drifted down, completely covering this corner of the lake and concealing all but the summits of the rocks.

THE BRIDGE-SPANNED GORGE BELOW THE VICTORIA FALLS

Below the world-famous Victoria Falls the River Zambezi flows for 40 miles through a sombre canyon, the walls of which are over 400 feet deep. The Victoria Falls Bridge across this canyon is an important link in the Cape to Cairo railway scheme. Completed in 1905, it forms a single majestic span 500 feet in length and standing 400 feet above the river. This picture shows its bold leap across the chasm.

THE VAST STRETCH OF THE VICTORIA

Rival in grandeur to Niagara, and surpassed only by the Iguazu Falls of South America, the Victoria Falls are formed by the great River Zambezi, about midway in its course through Central Africa. At a spot where the river is 1,860 yards wide, it drops in a thunderous roar perpendicularly over the edge of

E.N.A.

FALLS—AFRICA'S RIVAL TO NIAGARA

a chasm, amid clouds of mist and spray. The height of the fall varies from 200 to 355 feet. From the great chasm into which it is thus projected the river escapes by a single outlet at right angles to the falls, a gorge less than 100 feet wide, to continue its course through a sombre canyon, in places 400 feet deep.

E.N.A.

THE SUMMIT OF "WORLD'S VIEW"—LAST RESTING PLACE OF AN EMPIRE BUILDER

In the Matoppo Hills, a vast tract of granite rock some 100 miles long and 25 miles wide, about 10 miles from Bulawayo, is to be found this boulder-studded hill-top known as the "World's View." Some of these enormous boulders weigh over 100 tons and they were deposited there by long-passed glaciers. Cecil Rhodes, the founder of Rhodesia, was buried here and his grave is just visible on the left of the picture.

Ewing Galloway

VAST BRICKWORK RUINS OF A VANISHED CIVILIZATION

The famous ruins of Zimbabwe, situated near Victoria, in Mashonaland, were discovered in 1868 and their origin and meaning have long perplexed archæologists. While some authorities maintain they are of immense age, others claim that they date from the fifteenth century, and are the capital of the negro kingdom of Monomotapa. Here is seen a section of the enormous main wall, built of dried bricks, 30 feet high.

High Commissioner for Southern Rhodesia

GRACEFUL SPAN OF AFRICA'S LARGEST SUSPENSION BRIDGE

Presented by the Beit Trustees to the people of Southern Rhodesia, the Birchenough Road Bridge over the River Sabi was completed in 1935. Some 1,080 feet in clear span, and 300 feet above the river-bed, it is the third largest suspension bridge in the world, and was named in honour of the President of the British South Africa Co. The total cost of building this elegant structure was over £125,000.

E.N.A.

SLANGKOP, FAMOUS LANDMARK FOR DESERT TRAVELLERS

South Africa is noted for the fantastic forms often assumed by its "kopjes" or small hills. But none is stranger than Slangkop, this curiously crowned hill near Keetmanshoop in the former German colony of South-West Africa. Its distinctive shape makes it invaluable as a landmark for travellers, to many of whom, lost in the arid deserts forming a large proportion of the country, it has spelt salvation.

South African Railways

A POOL WHICH NO ONE HAS FATHOMED

South-West Africa, formerly a German possession, is now administered by the Union of South Africa. Large tracts of the country are arid desert, for the most part entirely devoid of water. This strange pool near Tsumeb, the northernmost railhead of the territory, is a remarkable exception. Although of small size it is of enormous depth and never appears to diminish. All efforts to plumb it have so far failed.

South African Railways

TRANSVAAL'S PREMIER DIAMOND MINE

Of all the diamond mines for which the Transvaal is famous the oldest and largest is the Premier Mine, 20 miles north-east of Pretoria, started in 1903. The area of its diamond-bearing vein is estimated at 350,000 square yards. It was in this mine, soon after opening, that the "Cullinan," largest diamond in the world (3,025$\frac{3}{4}$ carats, i.e., more than a pound and a half), was discovered on January 27, 1905.

South African Railways

A WALL WHICH HOLDS IN SIX AND A HALF SQUARE MILES WATER

The Hartebeestpoort Dam, near Pretoria, impounds water from the Crocodile River sufficient to irrigate over 30,000 acres of land in an area of some 250 square miles. The area of the reservoir formed when the dam is filled to capacity is 6½ square miles. This picture shows the principal wall of the dam.

South African Railways

BARREN HILLS OF WHITE DUST AND THE GREAT CITY THEY HAVE CREATED

Johannesburg, already a great modern city of over 600,000 inhabitants, owes its existence to the discovery of the world's greatest goldfields on the Witwatersrand in 1886. This general view, showing the city's striking skyline, is taken from the dumps of white dust from the mines, refuse of the crushing machines. These extend over the high veld for more than fifty miles, and no vegetation can be grown on them.

South African Railways

MAJESTIC ROCK SCENERY IN THE DRAKENSBERGS

Of all the magnificent rock scenery in which South Africa is so rich, none excels that to be found in the lofty Drakensberg Range. This picture shows a striking and famous view taken from the top of one of the flat-topped, precipitous escarpments of the Platberg, which forms a part of the Drakensberg system. The viewpoint overlooks the valley in the Orange Free State in which lies the health resort of Harrismith.

A FLOOD-LIT FAIRYLAND—THE

None of the many wonders which nature has wrought in South Africa excels in beauty the celebrated Cango Caves, which are situated in an outcrop of limestone amid the grandeur of the Zwartberg Mountains. They were first discovered in 1780 and have been explored for a distance of over two miles, but they extend much farther. The principal caverns have been skilfully flood-lit by electricity which has set off to

South African Railways

FANTASTIC PILLARS OF THE CANGO CAVES

perfection the fantastic and scintillating loveliness of the great stalagmites and stalactites, which are acclaimed as some of the finest in the world. This picture shows some of the lofty, fairy-like chambers in one of the chief caverns, Botha's Hall. Additional interest lies in a number of primitive Bushman wall-paintings, depicting a variety of subjects, including battle and hunting scenes, all drawn with great skill.

South African Railways

A SUPERB MEMORIAL TO AN EMPIRE BUILDER

At Rondebosch, a suburb of Cape Town, stands the national monument to Cecil Rhodes, the great South Africa statesman. The centrepiece of the memorial consists of G. F. Watts's famous bronze sculpture of " Physical Energy," a copy of which is to be seen in Kensington Gardens, London. The white granite structure, in a majestic setting, has been described as " one of the noblest monuments of modern times."

E.N.A.

TO THE TOP OF TABLE MOUNTAIN BY AERIAL RAILWAY

The summit of Table Mountain can now be reached in forty-five minutes from Cape Town Harbour. From the foot of the mountain an aerial cableway ascends to the hotel on the summit in eight minutes. Constructed in 1929 it is a magnificent feat of engineering, for the journey is taken in one span, on cables 4,000 feet long. This view shows a car leaving the top and, on the right, the famous Lion's Head Hill.

Fox

ETERNAL GUARD OVER CAPE TOWN

of the flat-topped hills that are such a characteristic feature of South African scenery. It extends like a great wall, 2 miles in length, behind the city, and its precipitous sides rise to a height of more than 3,500 feet above the level of the sea. The celebrated " Table Cloth " is formed by masses of white cloud which usually cling round the flat summit of the mountain. The mountain is a magnificent landmark for miles.

South African Railways

E.N.A.

WHERE NATURE HAS SCULPTURED THE BRITISH BOBBY

Few freaks of nature excel in quaintness this noteworthy rock formation known as "The Policeman's Helmet." Carved out of the volcanic rock by the action of wind and weather over countless centuries, it stands in the Natal National Park, a large area at the foot of the Drakensberg Mountains which has been set aside partly as a Game Reserve and partly to protect its many world-famous scenic beauties.

THE ROARING CAULDRON OF THE INCANDU FALLS

The Incandu River, which rises in the Drakensberg Mountains, tumbles down with extraordinary rapidity to join the Buffalo a few miles beyond Newcastle. Not far from the town occur these striking falls. Although there is no precipitous drop—for innumerable jagged rocks break up the river until it resembles a seething cauldron of foam and spray—the impression is remarkably beautiful and even more awe-inspiring.

INDEX

INDEX

Reprinted 1958
Made and Printed in Great Britain by Richard Clay and Company, Ltd., Bungay, Suffolk
S.258.6R.R.